This is absolutely first rate, the b
read it, several times I thought t
this passage." And almost every time I thought that, he soon quoted it. But he went beyond that, quoting many sources I have not seen myself. Bergman's research touches on every major issue related to Lewis and Darwinism.

A few things he does not mention include the character of Weston who, in *Out of the Silent Planet*, reminds one of the theistic evolutionist Henri Bergson, trusting in natural selection and what it implies. Science also runs amok in *That Hideous Strength*. And in chapter 2 of my *Lewis Agonistes* I end the chapter by retelling a scene from the *Silver Chair* that offers a powerful argument against the evolutionary mindset. Also in that chapter I argue that in all of C. S. Lewis's best apologetics he identifies things that could not have evolved. An example is in his argument of the two meanings of "fear" in the introduction to *The Problem of Pain*, where Lewis shows that the leap from the fear of wild animals to the fear of the unknown is a qualitative (not a quantitative) leap. In many of my speeches I use this event as an analogy to those who attempt to confuse microevolution with macroevolution. Another example is the antievolution stance in the scene from *Silver Chair*. In short, I am very, very impressed by this work. Bergman has done something very important and timely, and I hope that this book will be read by many persons.

—Professor Louis A. Markos, PhD
Internationally recognized Lewis scholar
and author of four books on Lewis

What a happy surprise this book is! I was delighted to learn that C. S. Lewis rejected Darwinism in all its forms—certainly not a given in his day, before the modern creation science movement had begun amassing evidence that the Genesis account of our origins is true. Dr. Bergman has done a masterful (and highly entertaining) job of documenting Lewis's unfolding thoughts on the subject and proving that he was indeed an increasingly belligerent opponent of evolution theory.

—Kitty Foth-Regner
Author of *Heaven Without Her: A Desperate Daughter's Search for the Heart of Her Mother's Faith*

Dr. Bergman, in his inimitable style, has surfaced otherwise suppressed or not-easily-attainable historical information regarding C. S. Lewis's personal stance on creation versus evolution. It is of tremendous importance where each of us, individually, "hangs our hat" in regards to these foundational questions and worldviews in life. C. S. Lewis opened many people's eyes in his generation, and now beyond, to the tantamount urgency of taking the time to ponder and think on things of eternal significance. This new book by Dr. Bergman will help you understand how the great writer and theologian, C. S. Lewis, eventually came to his terms with "hanging his hat" on the truth that we are all accountable to a Divine Creator.

—**Bryce Gaudian**
Hayward, Minnesota
Development Manager for Agilis Corporation

C. S. Lewis: Anti-Darwinist

C. S. Lewis: Anti-Darwinist

A Careful Examination of the Development of His Views on Darwinism

Jerry Bergman

Foreword by Ellen Myers

Preface by Karl Priest

WIPF & STOCK · Eugene, Oregon

C. S. LEWIS: ANTI-DARWINIST
A Careful Examination of the Development of His Views on Darwinism

Wipf & Stock
An Imprint of Wipf and Stock Publishers
199 W. 8th Ave., Suite 3
Eugene, OR 97401

www.wipfandstock.com

PAPERBACK ISBN: 978-1-5326-0773-8
HARDCOVER ISBN: 978-1-5326-0775-2
EBOOK ISBN: 978-1-5326-0774-5

Manufactured in the U.S.A. NOVEMBER 2, 2016

To my students who taught me so much during
my almost half-century teaching career.

Contents

Foreword

by Ellen Myers

FOR MANY YEARS, I believed that C. S. Lewis had made an uneasy truce with modern evolutionism. My opinion was based on certain passages in *Mere Christianity* and *The Problem of Pain*, in which he drew on evolutionist theories to illustrate Christian beliefs. It always seemed that one as committed to the gospel as C. S. Lewis could not have been neutral on the issue of creation ex nihilo versus evolutionism. As I studied Lewis, I realized that he debunked modern arrogant unbelief based on evolution and guesswork which masquerades as "science" in his largely autobiographical *The Pilgrim's Regress*, the first book published after his conversion. He also made it clear that he had what he called emergent evolutionism, today called Darwinism, in mind when he put the following words in the mouth of foolish old "Mr. Enlightenment": "If you make the same guess often enough it ceases to be a guess and becomes a Scientific Fact." How appropriate these sarcastic words are now, over fifty years later, about evolutionist dogma.

Lewis's essay "Two Lectures" can only be called creationist apologetics. It contrasts an urbane lecture about "Evolution, development, the slow struggle upwards and onwards from crude and inchoate beginnings towards ever-increasing perfection and elaboration that appears to be the very formula of the whole Universe" with a Dream Lecturer pointing out that, as the "acorn comes from a full-grown oak, the Rocket comes, not from a still crude engine, but from something much more perfect than itself and much more complex, the mind of a man, and a man of genius."

Lewis's most explicit antievolutionist writing is found in his essay *The Funeral of a Great Myth*, the bulk of which deals with the mythological implications of evolutionism in a manner devastating to believers of such myths. He makes it very clear that evolution is merely a hypothesis; and he speculates about the grounds for accepting the hypothesis as largely metaphysical and the fulfillment of an "imaginative need." Lewis added sarcastically that "probably every age gets, within certain limits, the science it desires."

No overview of Lewis and evolution would be complete without reference to Lewis's portraits of lost and evil men in his science fiction trilogy, *Out of the Silent Planet*, *Perelandra*, and *That Hideous Strength*. From the cold contempt and unscrupulous exploitation of feeble-minded Harry and Weston in *Planet*, to Filostrato's experiment with a guillotined man's head and Wither's trancelike senility in a demon-made void in *Strength*, exists a wealth of prophetic realism about the end result of the emergent evolutionist worldview for its practitioners-victims. Most horrible of them all is Weston, "a convinced believer in emergent evolution . . . the goal towards which the whole cosmic process is moving. Call it a great, inscrutable Force, pouring up into us from the dark bases of being . . . your Devil and your God are both pictures of the same Force."

From these excerpts it is clear that Lewis was unalterably opposed to emergent evolutionism and would have gladly welcomed the rise of creation science in our own generation. Bergman's book has proved beyond question that my early conclusions about Lewis were correct.

Professor Ellen Myers, MA
Author and Teacher

Preface

by Karl Priest

As I read Dr. Bergman's latest work, *C. S. Lewis: Anti-Darwinist*, I thought that Dr. Bergman is more than just a "mild-mannered" professor. He has documented that Lewis had major concerns both about Darwinism and the potential harm that science could cause in modern society. Lewis has succeeded as have few others in causing Christianity to be discussed both seriously and publicly. Lewis is the number one best-selling Christian author and has contributed greatly to Christianity being discussed academically. He used intelligent design as a basis for his apologetics; and, like any Christian who does not hide his light under a bushel, Lewis is the target of God-haters. Dr. Bergman robustly rebuts those who claim that Lewis believed in evolutionism. With powerful documentation, Dr. Bergman shows that C. S. Lewis was not even remotely a true believer in evolutionism.

Some confusion as to where Lewis stood was created by his use of the word "evolution" in the context of spiritual or mental advancement. Examination of some of his statements in context and accounting for where Lewis was in his spiritual growth exclude the possibility that he ended up believing in theistic evolutionism. The more Lewis learned, the greater was his hostility toward evolutionism.

Lewis was reared as a nominal Christian, but after his mother's death professed atheism when he was only fifteen years old. His atheism was based on what he believed was the findings of science. Not being a scientist, he had to take those findings on trust, actually on the authority of the scientists.

He was at this time living, like so many people today, in a whirl of contradictions. He not only maintained that God did not exist, but was also very angry with God for not existing. He was equally angry with God for creating our world. Although he had doubts about evolution all along, after Lewis became a Christian he began to seriously question evolution.

Lewis was restrained in his public attacks on evolution because he did not have scientific credentials and because he felt it would hamper his main ministry of Christian apologetics. Like those who reject Darwinism today (especially scientists), Lewis worked in a hostile environment and came to take bitterness and rancor due to his opposition as a matter of course. Lewis correctly knew that modern science was based on God as the Creator, writing: "Men became scientific because they expected Law in Nature, and they expected Law in Nature because they believed in a Legislator."[1]

Rather than antiscience, Lewis was antiscientism. Scientism is the belief that modern science supplies the "only reliable method of knowledge about the world, and its corollary that scientists have the right to dictate a society's morals, religious beliefs, and even government policies merely because of their scientific expertise."[2] Using his skills as a writer and thinker, Lewis attacked scientism and evolutionism. He used the term "emergent evolution" to describe Darwinism and called it "pure hallucination" in his essay *The Funeral of a Great Myth.*

Using logic, Lewis concluded that if evolution was true, once the solar system existed, then the appearance of organic life on this planet was ultimately an accident,

> brought about by an accidental collision and the whole evolution of Man was an accident too. If so, then all our present thoughts are . . . the accidental by-product of the movement of atoms. . . . I see no reason for believing that

1. Lewis, *Miracles*, 110.
2. West, *Magician's Twin*, 12.

one accident should be able to give me a correct account of all the other accidents. It's like expecting that the accidental shape taken by the splash when you upset a milk jug should give you a correct account of how the jug was made.[3]

Lewis called evolution "the central and radical lie in the whole web of falsehood that now governs" modern civilization.[4] True Believers in Evolutionism believe that evolution explains everything: the stars, the galaxies, the solar system, the planets, and all life from amoeba to humans. Lewis explained that evolution is "not the logical result of what is vaguely called 'modern science,' but rather is a picture of reality that has resulted, not from empirical evidence, but from imagination, [and] most people believe in orthodox evolution on the basis of authority 'because the scientists say so' and not on the basis of fact and scientific knowledge."[5]

With common sense logic, Lewis pointed out that the adult human being was once an embryo, but the life of the embryo came from two adult human beings. He added, "Since the egg-bird-egg sequence leads us to no plausible beginning, is it not reasonable to look for the real origin somewhere outside (of the) sequence altogether?"[6] You have to go outside the sequence of inventions, into the world of men, to find the real originator of the invention, asking, "Is it not equally reasonable to look outside Nature for the real Originator of the natural order?"[7] He realized that there was never a time when nothing existed, otherwise nothing would exist now.

Lewis, humorously, but aptly explained the evolution myth as humans evolving from a weak, tiny spark of life that began amid the huge hostilities of the inanimate, the product of another millionth millionth chance, adding that even seventh graders understand the math involved in the millionth millionth chance.

3. Lewis, *Business of Heaven*, 97.
4. Lewis, *Collected Letters*, 3:138.
5. Lewis, *Mere Christianity*, 63.
6. Lewis, *God in the Dock*, 229.
7. Ibid.

Relating the evolution myth to a play, Lewis said it is a story "preceded by the most austere of all preludes: the infinite void, and matter restlessly moving to bring forth it knows not what."[8] He added that "the Myth gives us almost everything the imagination craves—irony, heroism, vastness, unity in multiplicity, and a tragic close. . . . That is why those of us who feel that the Myth is already dead for us must not make the mistake of trying to 'debunk' it in the wrong way. . . . It is our painful duty to wake the world from an enchantment."[9] He knew that the evolution myth "has great allies, its friends are propaganda, party cries, and bilge, and Man's incorrigible mind."[10]

Lewis used a great term, "biolatry," to aptly describe what True Believers in Evolutionism do when they make evolution into an intelligent force. Rhetorically, he asked, "Does the whole vast structure of modern naturalism depend, not on positive evidence but simply on an a priori metaphysical prejudice? Was it devised not to get the facts but to keep out God?"[11] Lewis correctly feared "what man might do to mankind" because of the view "that morality is relative and that moral standards have grown from mere impulses, from chemical reactions and responses which are in turn simply part of the irrational, blind development of organic life from the inorganic."[12]

He pointed out the satanic scheme embraced by penning the demon dialogue in his book *The Screwtape Letters*: "So inveterate is their appetite for Heaven that our best method, at this stage, of attaching them to earth is to make them believe that the earth can be turned into Heaven at some future date by politics or eugenics or 'science.'"[13] As we are now seeing the fanaticism over evolutionism, we can understand the prophetic statement of Lewis when he said, "I dread government in the name of science. That is how

8. Lewis, *Weight of Glory*, 79.

9. Lewis, *Christian Reflections*, 116.

10. Ibid., 115.

11. Lewis, *Weight of Glory*, 136.

12. Crowell, "Theme of the Harmful Effects of Science," 12.

13. Lewis, *Screwtape Letters*, 156.

tyrannies come in."[14] And come in they have. C. S. Lewis, although not a perfect man, toward the end of his life he was not an evolutionist in any form. *C. S. Lewis: Anti-Darwinist* provides ample ammunition to win that argument.

Dr. Jerry Bergman continues to muzzle the megalomaniacal True Believer in Evolutionism villains who could easily be compared to General Zod from DC Comics: always defeated, yet ever trying to win by any vile means. In fact, the comic book series *Infinite Earths* is as believable as evolutionism on our unique earth. That said, like the imaginary Zod, True Believers in Evolutionism have caused a lot of havoc and harm in the world. Thank God for giving us an intellectual warrior—a superhero, Dr. Jerry Bergman—who can resist the archenemies of truth and all that is good.

Karl Priest, MA

14. Lewis, *God in the Dock*, 315.

Acknowledgments

I GRATEFULLY ACKNOWLEDGE THE research and contributions of Marilyn Dauer, Graig Davis, Bryce Gaudian, Adrian Chira, Professor Wayne Frair, and the staff at Marion E. Wade Center at Wheaton College in Wheaton, Illinois. Last, and most important, is Fred L. Johnson, PhD who critically reviewed the entire manuscript.

Introduction

So much has been written about C. S. Lewis that it makes one wonder, "What could one more book add?" The answer, in this case, is a great deal. This is the only book that looks specifically at his view on the topic of evolution, creation, and the science establishment. In short, a clear case can be made that he rejected Darwinism and even rejected theistic evolution, especially toward the end of his life, and accepted basic creationism. Lewis also called evolutionism the great myth, developmentalism, emergence theory, and Wellsianity after a leading proponent of evolution, H. G. Wells.[1] This book was written partly in response to several critics who claimed that Lewis accepted macroevolution and would not agree, even in principle, with either intelligent design or creationism.[2] The key to understanding Lewis is that he believed

> "a sane man accepts or rejects any statement, not because he wants to or does not want to, but because the evidence seems to him good or bad." This statement encapsulates Lewis's approach to religion: Follow the evidence. The overarching project of Lewis's Christian writings is to make the case that the evidence leads to Christianity.[3]

1. Dickerson and O'Hara, *Narnia and the Fields of Arbol*, 162.
2. E.g., see Peterson, "C. S. Lewis on Evolution and Intelligent Design."
3. Wielenberg, *God and the Reach of Reason*, 56.

In short, "C. S. Lewis . . . believed in argument, in disputation, and in the dialectic of Reason because he believed that the main business of life was a bold hunt for truth."[4]

Lewis also feared that science would lead to "rejection of absolute standards and traditional, objective values" leaving

> no defense against what some men might do with the powers of science. His love of individual freedom and his appreciation for men as creatures of worth in God's sight caused him to fear what might be done to men if science, without the old values to restrain it, were to be given the power of government to enforce what a few men might plan for all the rest.[5]

This is exactly what has happened today in many areas, including the forced teaching of Darwinism in the schools and termination of teachers who cause students to question the validity of Darwinism.[6] In his book *The Abolition of Man*, Lewis described the debunking of traditional values that he observed "in education, in sociology, psychology, biology, and philosophy" where students are

> taught that values are nothing but subjective reactions depending on body chemistry and environment. Then he traced the process of the "Conquest of Nature" by which one phenomenon after another is reduced to a quantitative object . . . the mind, reason, and all human characteristics become "merely" objects in Nature when men study them as such, forgetting that there is mystery and reality which cannot by studied empirically.[7]

This prediction has also now been fulfilled in Western society. We also will refute the claim that Lewis rejected a particular kind of argument for God, namely the

4. Murphy, *C. S. Lewis*, 11.
5. Crowell, "Theme of the Harmful Effects of Science," iii.
6. Bergman, *Slaughter of the Dissidents*.
7. Crowell, "Theme of the Harmful Effects of Science," ii–iv.

> oldest, most popular, and most enduring types of theistic arguments on the market: the argument from design.... A key element of the argument from design is the idea that the observable universe has certain features that indicate intelligent design at work in its formation. This argument comes in many varieties and has had many defenders.... Lewis, interestingly, is no friend of the design argument either.[8]

In fact, as will be documented in the following pages, a main apologetic argument that Lewis used to defend his worldview was the design argument. Since his death in 1963, as a result of his dedicated private secretary Walter Hooper, many unpublished Lewis manuscripts have been published.[9] These manuscripts, some that he did not feel comfortable publishing in his lifetime, have helped enormously in clarifying Lewis's conclusions, not only about Darwinism, but also about the science establishment, many of which have proved to be prophetic for today's world. His real concerns have been borne out in striking ways during the last few decades, especially in the intelligent design and creation-evolution struggles.

One problem is so many different editions, reprints, and compilations exist of Lewis's writings that referencing his work can be very problematic. I counted over fifty different editions of *Mere Christianity* in English, and no doubt my count is incomplete. Furthermore, it has been reprinted in several compilations of Lewis. Also American, British, and other editions exist, which make finding some of the quotes referenced difficult. For this reason, the book title is often given to allow the reader to locate the quotations of concern in his or her own edition.

8. Wielenberg, *God and the Reach of Reason*, 57.

9. McGrath, *C. S. Lewis*, 367.

1

Lewis the Man

OXFORD UNIVERSITY PROFESSOR C. S. Lewis was one of the most important Christian apologists of the last century.[1] He was also a major writer of fiction.[2] Toward the end of his long career Lewis concluded that the modern theory of evolutionary naturalism, often called Darwinism in honor of the man who was one of the most important modern popularizers of evolution, is one of the most destructive ideas ever foisted on civilization.

Lewis called Darwinism "emergent evolution" to distinguish it from what scientists today refer to as microevolution, what creationists and others refer to as variation within the creation kind. He concluded emergent evolution was "pure hallucination."[3] Lewis explained that, for the practical experimental scientist, "evolution is purely a biological theorem," which only attempts to explain certain changes in life or the environment, and

> makes no cosmic statements, no metaphysical statements, no eschatological statements [as does Darwinism]. Granted that we now have minds we can trust, granted that organic life came to exist, it tries to explain, say, how a species that once had wings came to lose them. It explains this by the negative effect of environment

1. At Oxford he taught from October 1924 to June 1954, at Cambridge from June 1954 until the summer of 1963, when he resigned due to health problems. He died in November 22, 1963. Wielenberg makes a persuasive argument that Lewis was one of the most important Christian apologists of the last century in his *God and the Reach of Reason*.

2. See Kilby, "Into the Land of Imagination."

3. Lewis, *They Asked for a Paper*, 164; Lewis, *Weight of Glory*, 138.

> operating on small variations. *It does not in itself explain the origin of organic life, nor of the variations*, nor does it discuss the origin and validity of reason.[4]

The form of evolution that taxonomists often called microevolution, and that creationists refer to as variation within the Genesis kinds, Lewis accepted. Evolutionary naturalism and macroevolution, as interpreted by leading scientists, such as those who are members of the National Academy of Science, *do* make cosmic, metaphysical, and eschatological statements, whereas microevolution limits itself to what biologists can study, such as epigenetic modifications and the loss of biological organs or functions as typified by blind cave fish. Lewis rejected the former, the macroevolution idea, and accepted the latter, the study of microevolution.

Some of the many reasons Lewis gave for rejecting evolutionary naturalism, many of which Lewis detailed extensively in his writings, are summarized in the following chapters in this book. It is also very clear that Lewis would be very supportive of the intelligent design movement today. We will document that claims, such as those by Professor Michael Peterson, that Lewis accepted "evolution as a highly confirmed scientific theory,"[5] given the definition of orthodox evolution used by most scientists today, are powerfully refuted by Lewis's own words.

Orthodox evolution is often called Darwinism to differentiate it from the term evolution, which can refer to anything from the differences between a son and a father, to scientism. The term Darwinism is often used instead of evolution to make this distinction clear. A major reason why, is because Darwin's theory

> required believing in *philosophical materialism*, the conviction that matter is the stuff of all existence and that all mental and spiritual phenomena are its by-products. Darwinian evolution was not only purposeless but also heartless—a process in which . . . nature ruthlessly

4. Lewis, *Christian Reflections*, 107, emphasis added. This quote is part of the essay "The Funeral of a Great Myth."

5. Peterson, "C. S. Lewis on Evolution," 253. See also http://biologos.org/author/michael-l-peterson.

> eliminates the unfit. Suddenly, humanity was reduced to just one more species in a world that cared nothing for us. The great human mind was no more than a mass of evolving neurons. Worst of all, there was no divine plan to guide us.[6]

Darwin "was keenly aware that *admitting any purposefulness* whatsoever to the question of the origin of species would put his theory of natural selection on a very slippery slope" that would eventually lead to its rejection.[7] Darwin concluded that his theory of natural selection replaced God and was actually a god: "I speak of natural selection as an active power or Deity . . . it is difficult to avoid personifying the word Nature; but I mean by nature, only the aggregate action and product of many natural laws."[8] Furthermore,

> Darwin realized that it would weaken his whole argument if he permitted his account of evolution to stop short of the highest forms of intelligence. Once he admitted that God might have intervened in an act of special creation to make man's mind, others might argue. "In that case, why not also invoke the aid of God to explain the worm?"[9]

Darwin also clearly taught atheistic evolution, stressing, "I would give absolutely nothing for the theory of natural selection if it requires miraculous additions at any one stage of descent" and makes "my Deity 'Natural Selection' superfluous" which would "hold *the* Deity—if such there be—accountable for phenomena which are rightly attributed only to" natural selection.[10]

6. Levine and Miller, *Biology: Discovering Life*, 161, italics in original.

7. Turner, *Tinker's Accomplice*, 206, emphasis added.

8. Darwin, *Origin of Species*, 99.

9. Gruber, *Darwin on Man*, 202.

10. See Darwin, letter to Asa Gray, June 5, 1861, in *Correspondence*, vol. 9; Darwin, *Origin of Species*, 99; Darwin, *Correspondence*, 7:345; Moore, *Post-Darwinian Controversies*, 322.

2

Darwinism and Creationism

THIS VIEW OF DARWIN is the position of many leading scientists and dominates the scientific literature today. One example is from one of the most prominent scientists today, Francisco Ayala. Professor Ayala wrote that Darwin's greatest discovery was to prove that design does not require a designer because his theory dispensed with the need for any Intelligent Designer, i.e., God.[1] This is a major reason why the vast majority of prominent scientists are atheists.

A survey by Larson and Witham found that 93 percent of members of America's most elite body of scientists, the National Academy of Sciences, are agnostics or atheists, and only 7 percent believe in a personal God, which as of 2015 is close to the exact reverse for the American public as a whole.[2] The effects of evolution on theism, as defined for the purposes of this book, were effectively articulated by the leading evolutionary biologist today, Richard Dawkins. He explained in a 1996 meeting that occurred in the gardens of his old college at Cambridge, called Clare College, that he had interviewed his friend, Nobel Laureate Professor Watson, the discoverer of the structure of DNA. Dawkins

> asked Watson whether he knew many religious scientists today. He replied: "Virtually none. Occasionally I meet them, and I'm a bit embarrassed [laughs] because, you

1. Ayala, "Darwin's Greatest Discovery," 8567.
2. Larson and Witham, "Leading Scientists Still Reject God."

> know, I can't believe anyone [today] accepts truth by revelation."[3]

Darwinism explains design without the need for a designer; thus, if you accept Darwinism, no reason any longer exists to believe in God. The major reason people give for belief in God is that creation requires an intelligent creator. And once the need for a creator is negated, evolution is the only option.[4]

An example is a leading early Darwinist, Darwin's cousin Francis Galton. Galton, the founder of the eugenic movement, rejected theistic evolution after reading Darwin's 1859 book *The Origin of Species*, believing that "evolution was not divinely directed, and that man might just as easily evolve backward toward the apes as forward into the image of his once-fancied Creator. Man's true religious duty, therefore . . . should be to the deliberate and systematic forward evolution of the human species."[5]

Evolution refers to the evolution of life from a one-celled first cell and is used also to explain all of physical creation. According to this view, no need exists to invoke God anywhere because natural law, time, and chance can, and did, create everything. Evolution, its adherents believe, explains everything: the stars, the galaxies, the solar system, the planets, and all life from amoeba to humans. One of the most succinct and widely disseminated definitions of evolution by natural selection was by the late Cornell professor Carl Sagan, who wrote in his book *Cosmos* and in his highly successful film series, also titled *Cosmos*, "The cosmos is all that is or ever was or ever will be."[6] Richard Dawkins, in *The Blind Watchmaker*, defined evolution as

> the blind watchmaker, blind because it does not see ahead, does not plan consequences, has no purpose in view. Yet the living results of natural selection overwhelmingly impress us with the appearance of design as

3. Dawkins, *God Delusion*, 99.
4. Shermer, *How We Believe*, xiv.
5. Beavan, *Fingerprints*, 100.
6. Sagan, *Cosmos*, 4.

> if by a master watchmaker, impress us with the illusion of design and planning.[7]

One of the world's leading evolutionists, the late Professor Theodosius Dobzhansky, defined evolution as a theory that comprises all of

> the stages of the development of the universe: the cosmic, biological, and human or cultural developments. Attempts to restrict the concept of evolution to biology are gratuitous. Life is a product of the evolution of inorganic nature, and man is a product of the evolution of life.[8]

Sir Julian Huxley wrote that soon after Darwin the

> concept of evolution was soon extended into other than biological fields. Inorganic subjects such as the life-histories of stars and the formation of the chemical elements on the one hand, and on the other hand subjects like linguistics, social anthropology, and comparative law and religion, began to be studied from an evolutionary angle, until today we are enabled to see evolution as a universal and all-pervading process.[9]

It is clear, as we will document, that Lewis openly rejected this orthodox view of evolution, the view that natural forces ultimately account for the creation of everything in the universe. Lewis wrote, "Deepening distrust and final abandonment of [evolutionary cosmology] long preceded my conversion to Christianity. Long before I believed Theology to be true I had already decided that the popular scientific picture [of evolutionary cosmology] . . . was false."[10]

His conversion was so important to him and his readers that Lewis wrote that his autobiography was written partly in answer to the many requests for him to explain how he progressed from Atheism to Christianity.[11] He added that his focus in his autobi-

7. Dawkins, *Blind Watchmaker*, 21.
8. Dobzhansky, "Changing Man," 409–15.
9. Huxley, "Evolution and Genetics," 272.
10. Lewis, "Is Theology Poetry?," in *They Asked for a Paper*, 162.
11. Lewis, *Surprised by Joy*, vii.

ography is "telling the story of my conversion and is not a general autobiography, still less 'confessions.'"[12]

Another term that must be discussed is creationism, which usually refers to the creation of all life kinds by God as outlined in the book of Genesis of the Bible. A more restrictive definition includes the belief in a flood that was universal in its extent and effect and in a young earth, from six to ten thousand years old. I was unable to find any direct reference to these ideas, either pro or con, in Lewis's writings or those of his associates who wrote about Lewis and thus cannot make a judgment on his views in this area.

Intelligent design did not exist as an organized movement when Lewis was alive, but he did make many statements related to this worldview that help to determine if he would have accepted this view were he alive today. Nonetheless, many creationists, such as many supporters of intelligent design, reject the evolution of all life from a common ancestor, but do not take a firm stand on the global flood and age of the earth issues.

Intelligent design focuses on evidence for intelligence in the natural world, such as the fact that the genomes existing in all life consist of information and the only known source of information is intelligence. Due to several court rulings,[13] the movement is often referred to as intelligent design creationism, confusing matters even more. To make matters even more difficult, Lewis *seemed* to waver a few times on the issue of origins, an issue that will be discussed in more detail in the text in this book.

A key focus of this book is on the conclusion that "Lewis consistently rejected one major feature of Darwinian evolution: its insistence on random, non-teleological processes . . . thus is much closer to Intelligent Design than to Darwinism."[14]

12. Ibid.

13. Such as that in Pennsylvania Tammy Kitzmiller, et al. v. Dover Area School District, et al. (400 F. Supp. 2d 707, Docket No. 4cv2688).

14. Weikert, "C. S. Lewis and Science," 1.

3

Lewis's Background

CLIVE STAPLES LEWIS WAS born in Belfast, Ireland, on November 29, 1898, to Albert James Lewis, a solicitor (a type of lawyer), and Florence Augusta Hamilton, a mathematician with a bachelor of arts degree from Queens College.[1] She was the daughter of a clergyman with many generations of clergymen and lawyers preceding her.[2] Both his parents were "bookish," and the home Lewis was reared in had

> books in the study, books in the drawing room, books in the cloakroom, books (two deep) in the great bookcase on the landing, books in a bedroom, books piled as high as my shoulder in the cistern attic, books of all kinds reflecting every transient stage of my parents' interest, books readable and unreadable, books suitable for a child and books most emphatically not. Nothing was forbidden me. In the seemingly endless rainy afternoons I took volume after volume from the shelves. I had always the same certainty of finding a book that was new to me as a man who walks into a field has of finding a new blade of grass.[3]

Lewis had one brother, Warren Hamilton, nicknamed Witt, who was Lewis's lifelong companion.[4] From this background came a legend. When C. S. Lewis died on November 22, 1963,

1. Dorsett, "C. S. Lewis."
2. Lewis, *Surprised by Joy*, 1.
3. Ibid., 7–8.
4. Gibb, *Light on C. S. Lewis*, vii.

the same day John F. Kennedy was assassinated, he was one of the most celebrated Christian apologists of the last century. Over a half-century after his death his books still sell several million copies annually.[5]

Lewis has also "succeeded as few others in causing Christianity to be discussed seriously and publicly."[6] A survey of 101 church leaders found that Lewis's book *Mere Christianity* was in the list of the top ten most influential books they have ever read.[7] He has also been called "one of the most brilliant minds of the 20th century."[8]

His Educational Background

Lewis earned a triple first class degree in philosophy from Oxford University. He was also fluent in six languages.[9] His mother began teaching him Latin and French when he was around eight, and he added Greek, Italian, and German as he got older.[10] Language skills are critical as a professor of literature. He published 125 essays and pamphlets, mostly on literary criticism and Christian apologetics.[11] As of this writing, Lewis is the best-selling Christian author of all time.[12] His twenty-nine BBC lectures given during World War II reached an audience estimated at 600,000.[13]

No narrow specialist, Lewis wrote about a remarkably wide range of subjects.[14] He penned nine books and about thirty essays that explored science and its impact on our modern culture.[15] All

5. Yancey, *What Good Is God?*, 100.
6. Deasy, "God, Space, and C. S. Lewis," 421.
7. Rainer, *Surprising Insights*, 149.
8. Crowell, "Theme of the Harmful Effects of Science," 4.
9. Ibid.
10. White, *Image of Man in C. S. Lewis*, 25.
11. Tolson, "God's Storyteller," 48; Reid, *Dictionary of Christianity*, 645.
12. Ibid.
13. Walsh, *C. S. Lewis*, 9.
14. Bredvold, "Achievement of C. S. Lewis," 1.
15. West, *Magician's Twin*, 11.

total, he produced forty-nine major titles from 1919 to 1967, including some titles published posthumously, an output level that was "astonishingly large" for a full-time professor.[16] These include the last book Lewis wrote, *The Discarded Image*, that

> critically examined the nature of scientific revolutions, especially the Darwinian revolution in biology. Lewis's personal library, meanwhile, contained more than three dozen books and pamphlets on scientific subjects, many of them dealing with the topic of evolution. Several of these books were marked up with underlining and annotations, including Lewis's copy of Charles Darwin's *Autobiography*.[17]

His Profession

C. S. Lewis was a professor for almost forty years, from 1925 until his premature death at age sixty-four in 1963.[18] He was a professor of medieval and early modern English literature, first at Oxford University, then at Cambridge University. He also was one of the "few dons whose lectures were always filled to overflowing."[19] As the stereotypical professor, he once said that it is "important to acquire early in life the power of reading . . . wherever you happen to be."[20]

In spite of the fact that he was the author of several highly acclaimed scholarly works of literary history and that his lectures were among the most widely attended at Oxford University, Oxford never promoted him to professor. As a result,

> Magdalen's brightest star was forced to slave away at time-consuming tutorials while many of his less brilliant colleagues were expected only to give lectures, thus freeing them up for research and publication. Still, this did

16. White, *Image of Man*, 21.
17. West, *Magician's Twin*, 11.
18. Tolson, "God's Storyteller," 46.
19. Crowell, "Theme of the Harmful Effects of Science," 4.
20. Lewis, *Surprised by Joy*, 53–54.

> not deter Lewis from producing a steady stream of popular and academic works as well as giving public lectures at numerous venues.[21]

Why he was not promoted was probably because "Lewis's refusal to hide his Christian faith under a bushel hurt his chances for promotion."[22] A problem was that "Lewis was unaware of quite how unpopular he was in the English Faculty at Oxford, and indeed in the University at large."[23] Consequently, there was

> no chance of his being elected to the Merton Chair even though *The Allegory of Love* and *A Preface to 'Paradise Lost'* (quite apart from other lectures and learned articles which he had written to date) were far more interesting and distinguished than anything which his rivals for the job had produced. They, however, were safe men, worthy dullards: and that is usually the sort of man that dons will promote.[24]

Another important factor was because

> Lewis had committed the unpardonable sin of being popular and reaching out to nonacademic readers. To make matters worse, he had spoken and published on subjects (like theology) that were outside his discipline. To be a generalist, and a popular one at that, was to fall foul of the rules of the club (dare I say inner ring?). Despite the advocacy of Tolkien, Lewis was unable to secure a professorship at Oxford.[25]

Yet another reason may be because "Oxford is a strange place, and dons are strange people. Brilliance in a colleague is quite as likely to excite their envy as their esteem, and, where mediocrity is the

21. Markos and Diener, *C. S. Lewis*, 20.
22. Ibid.
23. Wilson, *C. S. Lewis*, 208.
24. Ibid.
25. Markos and Diener, *C. S. Lewis*, 20.

norm, it is not long before mediocrity becomes the ideal."[26] For these reasons the

> Merton Chair of English Literature was to elude Lewis. In 1947 its occupant, David Nicholl Smith, retired, and Lewis assumed that he would be at least eligible, if not the likeliest candidate. He was weary of the repetitive round of undergraduate tutorials, and he disliked his colleagues at Magdalen. But even apart from these negative considerations, he considered himself worthy of the job. He was a popular and distinguished lecturer; and the job of an Oxford professor consisted very largely of lecturing in those days.[27]

In the end, it "was not Lewis but his old tutor, F. P. Wilson, who got the Merton Chair in 1947."[28] Wilson was a

> Shakespearean scholar who could be relied upon not to cause trouble, and not to embarrass his colleagues by writing books about Christianity. Even colleagues who were Christians found Lewis's career as a popularizer embarrassing. . . . And they noticed that his variety of Christianity did not extend to meekness, or even necessarily to politeness.[29]

Fortunately, just

> when Lewis had all but given up hope, Cambridge University came to the rescue and offered Lewis a professorship that they had created specifically to honor his work: a chair of medieval and Renaissance literature. . . . Lewis accepted the chair and held it from 1954 until his death in 1963. (Ironically, the college he worked for at Cambridge was [also] called Magdalene.)[30]

26. Wilson, *C. S. Lewis*, 208.
27. Ibid.
28. Ibid.
29. Ibid.
30. Markos and Diener, *C. S. Lewis*, 20.

Also, ironically, his love for Oxford was so great that on weekends he lived at his Oxford home in the Kilns.

He Becomes an Atheist

Although reared a nominal Christian, Lewis became an atheist at age fifteen due in part to his life experiences, such as the death of his mother when Lewis was still a young boy, and the arguments that he learned in school against the main proof of God, namely the cosmological argument. He writes that this conversation occurred at Chartres, the name he used for the Cherbourg School where he attended from January 1911 to June 1913. It was there that he made his first real friends. Lewis added that at Chartres "something far more important happened" to him, he

> ceased to be a Christian. The chronology of this disaster is a little vague, but I know for certain that it had not begun when I went there and that the process was complete very shortly after I left. I will try to set down what I know of the conscious causes and what I suspect of the unconscious.[31]

An important reason for his atheism was his "steadily growing doubts about Christianity."[32] He was also influenced by the then popular claim that life was poorly designed—a view now called dysteleology—and by certain evolutionists, such as the ancient Greek philosopher Lucretius. Lewis wrote in his autobiography that "the atheism of his early years on the faculty at Oxford University" was due to science. Specifically he wrote that

> "my [atheism] was inevitably based on what I believed to be the findings of the sciences; and those findings, not being a scientist, I had to take on trust, in fact, on authority." What Lewis is saying is that somebody told him

31. Lewis, *Surprised by Joy*, 55.

32. Ibid., 72.

> that science had disproved God; and he believed it, even though he knew [little] . . . about science.[33]

Lewis writes that, in his words, his

> early reading—not only [H. G.] Wells but Sir Robert Ball—had lodged very firmly in my imagination the vastness of cold and space, the littleness of Man. It is not strange that I should feel the universe to be a menacing and unfriendly place. Several years before I read Lucretius I felt the force of his argument (and it is surely the strongest of all) for atheism. . . . *Had God designed the world, it would not be a world so frail and faulty as we see.*[34]

He then combined this directly atheistical thought with this great "'Argument from Undesign' . . . that both made against Christianity."[35] Lewis wrote, "And so, little by little . . . I became an apostate, dropping my faith with no sense of loss but with the greatest relief."[36] Much later in his life, after much reading and study, he had a very different attitude about science, writing that the Renaissance was not about the return to Greek science and empiricism as commonly believed, but rather was in fact more like a

> golden age of magic and occultism. Modern writers who talk of "medieval superstitions" "surviving" amidst the growth of the "scientific spirit" are wide of the mark. Magic and "science" are twins *et pour cause*, for the magician and the scientist both stand together, and in contrast to the Christian.[37]

His longtime close associate Walter Hooper wrote that to appreciate Lewis's impact on Great Britain requires understanding the context in which he (Lewis) wrote, adding that "for centuries the heart of traditional Christianity had lain in the historic Incarnation, the belief that God became Man, but by the time Lewis was

33. Hooper, *C. S. Lewis*, 23.
34. Lewis, *Surprised by Joy*, 61–62, italics in original.
35. Ibid, 62.
36. Ibid.
37. Lewis, *Collected Letters*, 2:68.

converted to Christianity in 1931, Agnosticism was everywhere."[38] So was his belief in nothing existed "but atoms and evolution," which explained everything.[39] The result was his belief that the

> reliability of biblical scholarship had been punctured a good many years before by a number of things, amongst which were those "prophets of enlightenment": Charles Darwin, Karl Marx, Friedrich Nietzsche, Sigmund Freud, and Émile Durkheim—all of whose works Lewis . . . probably [was] . . . introduced to.[40]

Markos wrote that, until Lewis's 1931 conversion from atheism, he

> accepted without question the modernist paradigm. But after that life-altering event that transformed Lewis in heart, mind, and soul, he began slowly to question and doubt the evolutionary presuppositions upon which all of his previous knowledge had rested. Indeed, again and again in his major apologetical works, Lewis confronts his readers with a series of human phenomena that could not have evolved—that is to say, that could not have arisen from natural, material causes alone. At present, there are many Christian scholars and writers who have uncovered flaws in Darwinian evolution.[41]

The three common interpretations of Lewis's views of evolution, as defined above, include:

1. He was a theistic evolutionist after he left atheism. This is the view of Michael Peterson and others.
2. He was a theistic evolutionist after he left atheism, but became increasingly hostile to evolution in his later years.
3. He rejected theistic evolution for most of his life, although he may have flirted with some evolution ideas, not necessarily because he agreed with them, but to make the point that

38. Hooper, *C. S. Lewis*, 23.
39. Lewis, *Surprised by Joy*, 167.
40. Hooper, *C. S. Lewis*, 23.
41. Markos, *Lewis Agonistes*, 40.

Christianity could conceivably fit with some forms of theistic evolution.

This book focuses on positions 2 and 3 and concludes that the evidence best supports view 3. How well we succeed, the reader will have to judge. Lewis is said to never side-step tough issues, but for reasons that we will explain, it took him years to take Darwinism head on.[42] It also took him years to openly confront his atheism. One feature in the book *Loki Bound* worth commenting on is its pessimism: "I was at this time living, like so many Atheists or Antitheists, in a whirl of contradictions. I maintained that God did not exist. I was also very angry with God for not existing. I was equally angry with Him for creating a world."[43] Furthermore, he wrote that his

> rationalism was inevitably based on what I believed to be the findings of the sciences, and those findings, not being a scientist, I had to take on trust—in fact, on authority. Well, here was an opposite authority. If he had been a Christian I should have discounted his testimony, for I thought I had the Christians "placed" and disposed of forever. But I now learned that there were people, not traditionally orthodox, who nevertheless rejected the whole Materialist philosophy out of hand. . . . I [at the time] had no conception of the amount of nonsense written and printed in the world.[44]

42. Reid, *Dictionary of Christianity*, 645.

43. Lewis, *Surprised by Joy*, 110.

44. Ibid., 168.

4

His Return to Christianity and Opposition to Darwinism

AFTER MUCH SELF SOUL-SEARCHING and intensive reading, at the young age of thirty-three Lewis crossed the great Rubicon and returned to Christianity. One critical factor in his conversion was his study of apologetics, including the writings of George MacDonald who used stories to convey Christian apologetics, just as Lewis would become famous for later. Lewis soon became the "leading popular Christian apologist of the twentieth century."[1] Although the "most widely read religious spokesman of our time . . . his main occupation was scholarship and university teaching."[2]

As he studied the evidence and learned about the problems with evolutionary theory, Lewis also increasingly rejected Darwinism. In a letter to Douglas Bush dated March 28, 1941, Lewis recognized that "Darwin . . . made an upheaval" in science and society greater than even Copernicus and Freud. Lewis was, for this reason, very concerned about Darwinism's effects on people and society.[3]

Professor Louis Markos, one of the leading Lewis scholars today and the author of several books on Lewis, plus a twelve-hour lecture audio series on C. S. Lewis with the Teaching Company titled *The Life and Writings of C. S. Lewis*, wrote that if Lewis "were alive today, he would be an ID (intelligent design) . . . [supporter

1. Tolson, "God's Storyteller," 48.
2. Bredvold, "Achievement of C. S. Lewis," 1.
3. Lewis, *Collected Letters*, 2:476.

and] would have seen the flaws in Darwin and probably taken up the ID cause."[4]

Professor Louis Markos', a University of Michigan PhD, books on Lewis, include *Restoring Beauty: The Good, the True, and the Beautiful in the Writings of C. S. Lewis*; *Lewis Agonistes: How C. S. Lewis Can Train Us to Wrestle with the Modern and Postmodern World*; and *On the Shoulders of Hobbits: The Road to Virtue with Tolkien and Lewis.*

According to Professor Markos, a major concern of Lewis was responding to those who attempt to explain all life "by the process of evolution."[5] Lewis concluded that these persons "fail to explain why and how that process would evolve in us a yearning for realities that lie outside that very process and that cannot be satisfied by it" such as the existence of an afterlife.[6] Furthermore, for his entire life "Lewis displayed a healthy skepticism of claims made in the name of science. He expressed this skepticism even before he was a Christian."[7] An example is

> while still an unbelieving undergraduate in 1922, he recorded in his diary a discussion with friends where they expressed their doubts about Freud. In 1925, he wrote his father about his gratitude toward philosophy for showing him "that the scientist and the materialist have not the last word." The next year he published his narrative poem *Dymer*, which offered a nightmarish vision of a totalitarian state that served "scientific food" and "chose for eugenic reasons who should mate."[8]

Another example is, in 1923, only a few months after he converted to Christianity, Lewis wrote to his brother about his concerns over the fact that the Rationalist Press Association was publishing

4. Markos, e-mail message to Jerry Bergman, dated September 12, 2012.
5. Markos, *Lewis Agonistes*, 41.
6. Ibid.
7. West, *Magician's Twin*, 11.
8. Ibid.

> cheap editions of scientific works they thought debunked religion. Lewis said their efforts reminded him of the remark of another writer "that a priest is a man who disseminates little lies in defense of great truth, and a scientist is a man who disseminates little truths in defense of a great lie."[9]

Professor Harold Bloom of Yale, an agnostic Jew who opposed Evangelicals and personally knew Lewis, even attending his lectures at Cambridge, wrote,

> Lewis's *Mere Christianity* is a perpetual best-seller among American Evangelical Christians. His attitude towards Evolution is a touch more sophisticated than theirs, but differs from Creationism only in degree, not in kind. Indeed, Intelligent Design is a kind of parody of Lewis's general view of a Christian cosmos.[10]

In a book on C. S. Lewis edited by Bloom he stated that he read some two dozen of the forty books that Lewis wrote, thus his conclusions are based on extensive firsthand knowledge of Lewis's writings.[11]

An analogy that Lewis used to support his non-evolutionary view in *Mere Christianity* which illustrated his support of intelligent design is

> God made us: invented us as a man invents an engine. . . . He Himself is the fuel our spirits were designed to burn, or the food our spirits were designed to feed on. . . . God cannot give us happiness and peace apart from Himself, because it is not there.[12]

Owen Barfield, who had known Lewis from the time of Lewis's return to Oxford after World War I, put it even more strongly, writing that Lewis "didn't believe in [Orthodox] evolution. . . . Now Lewis, as you know, hated the idea of evolution."[13]

9. Ibid., 11–12.
10. Bloom, *C. S. Lewis*, 2.
11. Ibid.
12. Lewis, *Mere Christianity*, 54.
13. Poe and Poe, *C. S. Lewis Remembered*, 104.

One of Lewis's doctoral students, Alastair Fowler, wrote that he (Fowler) occasionally had a few disagreements with Lewis, then his doctoral supervisor. One "concerned Charles Darwin; Lewis saw the theory of natural selection as threatening religion" whereas Fowler didn't. Fowler added, in their debates on evolution that he (Fowler) "grew as red as Lewis himself. But he [Lewis] nimbly reined in, avoiding the threatened collision; he never lost his temper in debate [with him about evolution]."[14]

It may have been this and similar experiences that caused Lewis to realize that, due to his lacking a good science background, it was difficult for him to debate evolution with someone like Fowler, who had an excellent science background.

A master of arts thesis completed on Lewis and science concluded that Lewis "later accepted the biblical view of man as being created in the image of God and, though fallen from the original position of fellowship with God [man was] . . . of such value that the Incarnation and the Crucifixion resulted."[15] The thesis concluded that Lewis taught, in contrast to Orthodox Darwinism, that

> naturalism, determinism, and empiricism all view man as a biological accident with no meaning and no unmeasurable qualities like soul or spirit. They presuppose that there is no God nor absolute truth or values. The study of man by sociologists, psychologists, and anthropologists has reduced him to a thing having little dignity or worth, having little or no individual responsibility for his choices and actions.[16]

Lewis's major concern was, in attempting to explain humans,

> scientists have "explained away" his value and meaning. This sort of explaining, or reductionism, is contemporary nihilism, according to Swiss psychiatrist Viktor Frankel, who blames the complaint of meaninglessness

14. Ibid.

15. Crowell, "Theme of the Harmful Effects of Science," 73.

16. Ibid., 74.

> heard from his patients on those who say "time and again that something is nothing but something else."[17]

Along with reductionism, "Lewis also deplored the arrogance of some scientists and philosophers who insist that only that which may be verified empirically is true and real."[18]

DePaw University president Erik Wielenberg wrote that it is clear in Lewis's writings that he accepted the design argument for God. Lewis's case for Christianity and God contains two main components. The first

> consists of arguments for the claim that there is, in addition to the natural, physical universe that we perceive with our senses, some transcendent being, a Higher Power that created the natural universe and is "more like a mind than it is like anything else we know."[19]

On May 13, 1943, the well-known Christian author Dorothy Leight Sayers (1893–1957), wrote to thank Lewis for the insight that she gleaned from his writings.[20] In her letter, she also complained about an atheist who was communicating with her about his problems relating to the validity of Christianity. She then asked Lewis if there existed

> any up-to-date books about Miracles. People have stopped arguing about them. Why? Has Physics sold the pass? . . . Please tell me what to do with this relic [of the atheists] of the Darwinian age who is wasting my time, sapping my energies, and destroying my soul.[21]

This communication was one factor of several that motivated Lewis to begin his lifelong apologetics career. This career helped to birth his concerns about evolution that grew as he grew older. As will be documented, Lewis had major doubts about Darwinism

17. Frankel, "Nothing But—," 54.

18. Crowell, "Theme of the Harmful Effects of Science," 74.

19. Wielenberg, *God and the Reach of Reason*, 56.

20. She is most well known in theology for her 1941 book *The Mind of the Maker* (HarperOne; repr. 1987).

21. Quoted in Hooper, *C. S. Lewis*, 343.

not long after he became a believer, and these concerns became stronger as he researched the issue.

As early as 1927, after quoting a nineteenth-century scientist, he wrote in a letter to his father, dated March 30, about evolution, in which he stated that "you need more *faith* in science than in . . . theology."[22] A review of a book on Lewis and science edited by John West explored Lewis's views on Darwinism in this book. West lays to rest the myth that Lewis was a gung-ho theistic evolutionist."[23] West acknowledges that at one time in his life Lewis evidently

> accepted the plausibility of some kind of common descent. However, later in life he became more skeptical about any form of evolution, though. . . . Two of the most interesting findings by West are: (1) that Lewis was skeptical of Darwinism before he even converted to Christianity; and (2) that Lewis consistently rejected one major feature of Darwinian evolution: its insistence on random, nonteleological processes. Even when he accepted the possibility of common ancestry, he always rejected the notion that the process could have been random. West argues that Lewis's position is thus much closer to Intelligent Design than to Darwinism.[24]

This brief review is a good summary of Lewis's lifelong attempt to grapple with the whole Darwin evolution issue.

22. Lewis, *Collected Letters*, 1:680.

23. Weikart, "C. S. Lewis and Science."

24. Ibid.

5

A Harvard Scholar's View on Lewis

HARVARD UNIVERSITY PROFESSOR OF psychiatry Armand M. Nicholi has for over thirty years taught a course on Freud's person and ideas. The class eventually morphed into a course on both Freud and C. S. Lewis.[1] Dr. Nicholi later wrote a book based on his Harvard course contrasting and comparing the worldviews of these two intellectual giants. As is obvious from his textbook, Professor Nicholi is an expert on both men.

Professor Nicholi noted that both were reared in a religious environment, specifically Christian,[2] both became atheists as adolescents, and both spent the rest of their lives proselytizing, Freud for atheism and Lewis for theism, specifically Christianity. Nicholi documents how important intelligent design was in Lewis's conversion. In a chapter of his book titled "The Creator: Is There an Intelligence beyond the Universe," Nicholi writes that as

> an atheist, Lewis agreed with Freud that the universe is all that exists—simply an accident that just happened. But eventually Lewis wondered whether its incredible vastness, its precision and order, and its enormous complexity reflected some kind of Intelligence. Is there Someone beyond the universe who created it? Freud answers this "most important question" with a resounding "No!" The very idea of "an idealized Superman" in the sky—to use Freud's phrase—is "so patently infantile and

1. Nicholi, *Question of God*, 5.

2. Freud was born to Jewish German parents, but went to a Catholic school and converted to Christianity.

> so foreign to reality, that . . . it is painful to think that the great majority of mortals will never rise above this view of life."[3]

Freud predicted that, as the average common people became better "educated, they would 'turn away' from 'the fairy tales of religion.' He reminds us that 'the world is no nursery' and strongly advises us to face the harsh reality that we are alone in the universe."[4] In contrast, after his worldview changed, Lewis asserted

> that the universe is filled with "signposts" like the "starry heavens above and the moral law within"—Immanuel Kant's phrase—all pointing with unmistakable clarity to that Intelligence. Lewis advises us to open our eyes, to look around, and understand what we see. In short, Lewis shouts, "Wake up!"[5]

One fact that Nicholi notes deeply impressed Lewis, was his observation that "our physical universe . . . is extremely complex . . . it comprises atoms, electrons, etc." and "the universe is not just the sum of its physical parts" but much more.[6] This reasoning sounds very much like that espoused in the modern intelligent design movement. Conversely, Freud believed that evolutionary science has shown God is "so improbable, so incompatible with everything we had laboriously discovered about the reality of the world" by science.[7]

Lewis, a Respected Oxford Scholar

Lewis was not only a teacher and historian, but frequently published in both widely respected academic and nonacademic venues.[8] His doctoral student noted above, Alastair Fowler, observed

3. Nicholi, *Question of God*, 36.
4. Ibid.
5. Ibid., 36–37.
6. Ibid., 54.
7. Ibid., 55.
8. Hart, "Teacher, Historian, Critic, Apologist."

that Lewis's "scholarly and religious lives were really no more separable than two sides of the same coin."[9] Lewis existed in a hostile academic environment while at Oxford that was "resentful of his outspoken faith" and "denied him a full professorship . . . an injustice that rival Cambridge University later rectified," as noted previously, by appointing Lewis as a professor.[10] The few colleagues that he had an excellent relationship with included the fellow Christian J. R. R. Tolkien.[11]

Lewis was an enormously influential Christian apologetist in his day, and his popularity shows no sign of diminishing in ours.[12] Lewis's writings have been translated into thirty languages and have sold over forty million copies.

Lewis saw his mission as bringing a viable, vibrant Christianity to the post-Christian world by his lectures and many books, a goal that he has achieved beyond anyone's expectation, most of all his own.[13] Lewis's focus was "on the core of Christianity that was common to all traditional Christian denominations" which he called "mere Christianity."[14]

His Christian-based fiction book *The Lion, the Witch, and the Wardrobe*, which was part of his seven-volume *Chronicles of Narnia* series, was adapted for a major Hollywood film.[15] Lewis's *Mere Christianity*, *The Problem of Pain*, *The Screwtape Letters*, and *The Abolition of Man* are all still extremely popular and influential Christian apologetic works. In April of 2000, *Mere Christianity* was voted by *Christianity Today* as the best Christian book published in the twentieth-century.

Many persons who later became well-known Christians were converted from atheism as a result of the influence of Lewis's writings. These include former atheist Chuck Colson and leading

9. Poe and Poe, *C. S. Lewis Remembered*, 126.
10. Yancey, *What Good Is God?*, 95.
11. Glyer, *Company They Keep*.
12. Green, *C. S. Lewis*; Green and Hooper, *C. S. Lewis*.
13. Tolson, "God's Storyteller," 50.
14. Collins, *Did Adam and Eve Really Exist?*, 13.
15. Tolson, "God's Storyteller," 46.

genetic scientist Francis Collins, previously head of the Human Genome Project and currently director of the National Science Foundation.[16] The popular author Philip Yancey also acknowledged the critical influence of Lewis in his life. Yancey writes,

> Lewis taught me a style of approach that I try to follow in my own writing. Most of us rarely accept a logical argument unless it fits our sense of reality, and the persuasive writer must cultivate that intuitive sense—much as Lewis did for me with his space trilogy before I encountered his apologetics. I came to believe in the invisible world only after tracing its clues in the visible world. Lewis himself converted to Christianity only after sensing that it corresponded to his deepest longings, his Sehnsucht [his "yearning" for more].[17]

Yancey's statement that Lewis "came to believe in the invisible world only after tracing its clues in the visible world" is significant in view of the focus of the book you are now reading. Likewise, many other modern apologists "have cut their eye teeth on Lewis's works."[18] So many examples exist that Andrew Lazo and Mary Anne Phemister conclude that "no author of the twentieth century has had a greater spiritual impact on more people than Lewis."[19] They collected a total number of accounts of fifty-five writers, professors, and others who were heavily influenced by Lewis, which they included in their book titled *Mere Christians: Inspiring Stories of Encounters with C. S. Lewis*. These notable persons included George Gallup Jr., Anne Rice, leading author Randy Alcorn, Liz Curtis Higgs, Walter Hooper, Thomas Howard, Jill Briscoe, and David Lyle Jeffrey.

One notable example of a person impacted by Lewis was a poet and novelist named Helen Joy Davidman Gresham (1915–1960). When Lewis was in his early fifties, he struck up a correspondence

16. Collins, *Did Adam and Eve Really Exist?*, 21.

17. Yancey, *What Good Is God?*, 94.

18. Markos, *Lewis Agonistes*, 42.

19. Quote is from the promotional material of Lazo and Phemister, *Mere Christians*, at Amazon.com.

with her. Joy was a "nonpracticing Jew from the Bronx," New York who had "been both an atheist and a communist."[20] Her reading of Lewis's apologetical works had helped lead her to faith in Christ. She visited

> Lewis in Oxford in 1952, and their friendship blossomed. Two years later, Joy was back in England with her two sons; she was now divorced from her alcoholic, serially unfaithful husband, and was getting by as best she could.[21]

As a young woman, like Lewis, Joy had also "assumed that science also proved that God didn't exist"[22] but traveled down a similar road that Lewis did and also eventually became a believer. Also like Lewis, she eventually "realized she had believed in science the way religious people believe in God [when she realized it was] illogical and, even worse, naïve, to believe that the wonders of the atom had evolved blindly out of chaos [as evolution teaches]."[23] She also concluded that false gods were "Sex, the State, Science, and Society," with "self" being the greatest god of all.[24] Thus, they had much in common and became soul mates, marrying in April of 1956. She turned out to be an important source of inspiration for both Lewis and his writing and was the subject of his book *A Grief Observed*. She tragically died of cancer at the young age of forty-five.

20. Markos and Diener, *C. S. Lewis*, 21; reprinted in Lewis, *They Asked for a Paper*.

21. Ibid.; reprinted in Lewis, *They Asked for a Paper*, 14.

22. Santamaria, *Joy*, 22.

23. Ibid., 175.

24. Ibid., 219.

6

Lewis Opposes Evolution and Naturalism

WHEN LEWIS MOVED TO Cambridge, his first lecture there argued that "the so-called divide between a dark and ignorant Middle Ages and an enlightened Renaissance is mostly fictitious, invented by modern thinkers eager to discredit medieval faith and thought" that brought the West to the post-Christian era.[1] As Lewis argued in this lecture, "Christians and Pagans had much more in common with each other than either has with a post-Christian. The gap between those who worship different gods is not so wide as that between those who worship and those who do not."[2] It is this gap that we will explore in this chapter.

Two topics of special concern to Lewis, especially when he was older and better informed on the subject, were orthodox materialistic Darwinism, which he came to regard as "a Great Myth," and "naturalism,"[3] the core of evolution.[4] He often referred to "naturalistic theories of evolutionary development" by the term *developmentalism*.[5] As will be discussed later, Lewis concluded

1. Lewis, "De Descriptione Temporum," 5; also reprinted in Lewis, *They Asked for a Paper*.

2. Ibid., 5; also reprinted in Lewis, *They Asked for a Paper*.

3. Martindale and Root, *Quotable Lewis*, 193–97.

4. Ayala, "Darwin's Greatest Discovery," 8567.

5. Lewis, *Collected Letters*, 3:1584.

that naturalism was self-refuting because it is contradicted by both fact and reason.[6]

In some of his early writings, such as *Mere Christianity*, Lewis appeared in places in his writing to accept some evolutionary ideas, at least in part. As he researched the subject, though, his writings eventually reflected a vivid opposition to the "Great Myth" of evolutionary naturalism. As Professors Ferngren and Numbers conclude, with study and reflection "Lewis grew increasingly uncomfortable with the claims being made for organic evolution."[7] Numbers added that, privately, Lewis found the

> arguments against evolution increasingly compelling—and the pretensions of many biologists repellent. In 1951 he confessed that his belief in the unimportance of evolution had been shaken while reading one of his friend's manuscripts. "I wish I were younger," he confided to [Bernard] Acworth. "What inclines me now to think that you may be right in regarding it [evolution] as *the* central and radical lie in the whole web of falsehood that now governs our lives is not so much your arguments against it as the fanatical and twisted attitudes of its defenders."[8]

Bernard Acworth (1885–1963), a "decorated World War I submariner and a pioneer in the development of sonar,"

> founded Britain's Evolution Protest Movement and published books criticizing evolution. It is not known when Acworth and C. S. Lewis first met, but the earliest of the ten surviving letters from Lewis to Acworth show that a warm friendship already existed in 1944, with Acworth sometimes staying with Lewis when he was in Oxford.[9]

Books that influenced Lewis's opposition to Darwinism include *The Everlasting Man*, first published in 1925 and written by one of the most well-known nineteenth-century antievolutionists,

6. Reppert, *C. S. Lewis's Dangerous Idea*.
7. Ferngren and Numbers, "C. S. Lewis on Creation and Evolution," 28.
8. Numbers, *Creationists*, 175.
9. Schultz et al., *Encyclopedia of Religion*, 69.

Gilbert Keith (G. K.) Chesterton (1874–1936). Evolutionist Martin Gardner called this book an antievolution missive that was written partly in rebuttal of Darwinism and especially of H. G. Wells's arguments for evolution as contained in his wildly successful book *Outline of History*.[10]

Gardner added that the *Everlasting Man* book argued that the enormous gap existing between humans and apes strongly speaks against human evolution.[11] Genetic analysis has shown that this gap actually is a chasm involving a difference of close to 360 million genetic base pairs.[12] Wells, in his *Outline*, argued for the evolutionary origin of humans, focusing on Darwin's conclusion that humans are quantitatively, but not qualitatively, higher than the animals.

Lewis viewed *The Everlasting Man* book as so important to his Christian walk that he credited it with moving him from his previous half-converted state to fully embracing orthodox conservative Christianity. As he wrote to educator Rhonda Bodle on December 31, 1947, "The very best popular defense of the full Christian position I know is G. K. Chesterton's *The Everlasting Man*."[13] As late as 1961, he still regarded this book as an excellent apologetic writing, adding that for "a good ('popular') defense of our position against modern woffle . . . , I know nothing better than G. K. Chesterton's *The Everlasting Man*."[14]

He first became aware of Chesterton's writings while in a hospital recovering from "trench fever" when serving during World War I, writing that this was when he

> first read a volume of Chesterton's essays. I had never heard of him and had no idea of what he stood for; nor can I quite understand why he made such an immediate conquest of me. It might have been expected that my pessimism, my atheism, and my hatred of sentiment

10. Gardner, *Fads & Fallacies*, 134.
11. Ibid.
12. Tomkins and Bergman, "Is the Human Genome."
13. Lewis, *Yours, Jack*, 125.
14. Lewis, *Joyful Christian*, 103.

> would have made him to me the least congenial of all authors. It would almost seem that Providence, or some "second cause" . . . , quite overrules our previous tastes when it decides to bring two minds together.[15]

He added, in reading Chesterton, as in reading Scottish writer and scholar George MacDonald (1824–1905), who believed that "all imaginative meaning originates with the Christian creator God,"[16] he "did not know what he was letting himself in for. A young man who wishes to remain a sound Atheist cannot be too careful of his reading."[17] In his words, when he read Chesterton's *Everlasting Man*, he

> for the first time saw the whole Christian outline of history set out in a form that seemed to me to make sense. Somehow I contrived not to be too badly shaken. . . . I already thought Chesterton the most sensible man alive "apart from his Christianity." Now I veritably believe, I thought—I didn't of course *say*; words would have revealed the nonsense—that Christianity itself was very sensible.[18]

In another letter dated December 14, 1950, to Oxford history graduate student Sheldon Vanauken, Lewis called *The Everlasting Man* "the best popular apologetic I know."[19] The book was also cited as number two in Lewis's list of the ten books that were the most important in shaping his Christian faith and philosophy of life.[20]

To prove his case for human evolution, Darwin penned the two-volume, nearly nine hundred-page book, *The Descent of Man*, that "forcefully argued that unguided natural selection could produce man's mental and moral faculties perfectly well. . . . Lewis thought otherwise, and he was tutored in his doubts by a book from of one of his favorite authors, G. K. Chesterton. The book was

15. Lewis, *Surprised by Joy*, 182–83.
16. Duriez, *A–Z of C. S. Lewis*, 183.
17. Lewis, *Surprised by Joy*, 183.
18. Ibid., 213.
19. Ibid., 154.
20. Lewis, "What Books."

Chesterton's *Everlasting Man*."[21] In chapter 2, titled "Professors and Prehistoric Men,"

> Chesterton skewered the pretensions of anthropologists who spun detailed theories about the culture and capabilities of primitive man based on a few flints and bones, likely inspiring Lewis's discussion of "the idolatry of artifacts" in *The Problem of Pain*. But Chesterton also provides in his book a full-throttled argument as to why Darwinism cannot explain the higher capabilities of man. In Chesterton's words, "Man is not merely an evolution but rather a revolution" whose rational faculties far outstrip those seen in the other animals.[22]

In a review of *C. S. Lewis's Dangerous Idea*, Baylor University professor of philosophy C. Stephen Evans wrote,

> Darwinists try to show through science that our world and its inhabitants can be fully explained as the product of a mindless, purposeless system of physics and chemistry. But as Victor Reppert explains . . . Lewis demonstrated that the Darwinian argument was circular: if such materialism or naturalism were true, then scientific reasoning itself could not be trusted. Reppert [demonstrates] . . . that—contrary to the dismissals of hasty critics—the basic thrust of Lewis's argument from reason can bear up under the weight of the most serious philosophical attacks.[23]

Evans concluded Reppert has documented the fact that

> Lewis's most tenacious critics don't even attempt to refute his arguments—instead, they simply resort to base *ad hominem* attacks aiming squarely at modern-day intellectuals who sneer at Lewis's arguments because he wasn't a credentialed philosopher, Reppert demonstrates that Lewis's powerful philosophical instincts perhaps ought to place him among those other thinkers who, by

21. West, *Magician's Twin*, 128.

22. Ibid.

23. Evans, "Body Blow."

> contemporary standards, were also amateurs: Socrates, Plato, Aristotle, Aquinas, Descartes, Spinoza, Locke, and Hume.[24]

Another author Lewis listed in the 1962 *Christian Century* article that had a major impact on him was Arthur J. Balfour, author of *Theism and Humanism*. This book was Balfour's 1914 Gifford lecture presented at the University of Glasgow. Balfour was one of Great Britain's most respected leaders, serving as prime minister from 1902 to 1905. Although most well known today for the Balfour Declaration, which established a homeland for the Jews in Palestine in 1948, he was a Christian apologist and outspoken anti-Darwinist whose ideas found in the Gifford lectures permeate the first five chapters of Lewis's book *Miracles*.[25]

After reviewing the theories of the leading evolutionist and social Darwinist Herbert Spencer, Balfour wrote that a major problem with Spencer's evolutionary ideas was "its central episode, the transition from the not-living to the living, was never explained by Spencer in his *Synthetic Philosophy*; and the lamentable gap must be filled in by each disciple according to his personal predilections. For the moment, however, we are concerned only with one part of the story."[26]

Balfour added, "Spencer himself was, of course, no advocate of 'design' after the manner of Paley; and I only mention his cosmic speculations because their unavowed optimism—the optimism that is always apt to lurk in the word 'evolution'—makes of them material peculiarly suitable for those who seek for marks of design in lifeless nature."[27]

After noting "the great omission which mars the continuity of his world-story—the omission . . . of any account of the transition from the not-living to the living . . . there are, besides this, two other omissions, one at the beginning of his narrative, and the

24. Ibid.
25. Balfour, *Theism and Humanism*.
26. Ibid., 28.
27. Ibid., 29.

other at the end, whose significance in relation to 'design' should receive a passing comment."[28]

Another problem for Darwinism that Balfour noted was "the argument from 'design'" which was "the foundation on which those who use the argument have chiefly built" have always sought for evidence of contrivance among life, such as

> the intricate adjustment of different parts of an organism to the interests of the whole; in the adaptation of that whole to its environment, they found the evidence they required. Arrangements which so irresistibly suggested purpose could not (they thought) be reasonably attributed to chance. . . . If we consider organic adaptations and adjustments in themselves, scientific discovery has increased a thousand-fold our sense of their exquisite nicety and their amazing complexity. I take it as certain that, had no such theory as Natural Selection been devised, nothing would have persuaded mankind that the organic world came into being unguided by intelligence. Chance, whatever chance may mean, would never have been accepted as a solution. Agnosticism would have been scouted as stupidity.[29]

Balfour, who knew Charles Darwin personally, wrote that what changed the view that was enumerated above, so that agnosticism was no longer regarded as "stupidity" by the intellectual class, was Charles Darwin, who

> is justly regarded as the greatest among the founders of the doctrine of organic evolution; but there is nothing in the mere idea of organic evolution which is incongruous with design. On the contrary, it almost suggests guidance, it has all the appearance of a plan. Why, then, has Natural Selection been supposed to shake teleology to its foundation?[30]

28. Ibid.
29. Ibid., 30.
30. Ibid., 30–31.

Balfour concluded, "Selection does not make it harder to believe in design, it makes it easier to believe in accident; and, as design and accident are the two mutually exclusive alternatives between which the argument from design requires us to choose, this comes to the same thing."[31] Thus, before Darwin "those who denied the existence of a Contriver [God] were hard put to it to explain the appearance of contrivance. Darwin . . . provided an explanation."[32] Furthermore, Balfour asked, could

> the most complicated and purposeful organs gradually arise out of random variations, continuously weeded by an unthinking process of elimination. Assume the existence of living organisms, however simple, let them multiply enough and vary enough, let their variations be heritable, then, if sufficient time be granted, all the rest will follow. In these conditions, and out of this material, blind causation will adapt means to ends with a wealth of ingenuity which we not only cannot equal, but which we are barely beginning to comprehend.[33]

Thus, Balfour opines, Darwin murdered the "Contriver," God. Balfour then concluded that the "theory of selection thus destroys much of the foundation on which, a hundred years ago, the argument from design was based. What does it leave untouched?"[34] He deals with this problem by observing that Natural

> Selection may modify these conditions, but it cannot start them. . . . It may enable organic species to adapt . . . but it cannot produce either the original environment or the original living matter. These must be due either to luck or to contrivance; and, if they be due to luck, the luck . . . is great. . . . We cannot measure the improbability of a fortuitous arrangement of molecules producing not

31. Ibid.
32. Ibid., 31.
33. Ibid.
34. Ibid.

> merely living matter, but living matter of the right kind, living matter on which selection can act.[35]

He added that suppose we measure

> the odds against the accidental emergence of the desired brand of protoplasm, how are we to compare this probability with its assumed alternative—intelligent design? Here, I think, even Laplace's calculator would fail us; for he is only at home in a material world governed by mechanical and physical laws. He has no principles which would enable him to make exhaustive inferences about a world in which other elements are included.[36]

Thus, Balfour notes, the problem Darwin had, which still is its major problem today, namely not the survival of the fittest, but rather the arrival of the fittest problem. He writes that "the progress either of science or philosophy" has not brought us closer to the solution of

> the argument from design. . . . Those who refuse to accept design do so because they think the world-story at least as intelligible without it as with it. This opinion is very commonly associated with [the idea that] . . . the laws of matter and energy are sufficient to explain, not only all that is, but all that has been or that will be. . . . The choice, therefore, is not between two accounts of the universe, each of which may conceivably be sufficient. The mechanical account . . . doubly fails to provide a satisfactory substitute for design.[37]

The reasons include the belief that Darwinism requires us to believe "that the extraordinary combination of material conditions required for organic life" is ultimately due to chance and the fact that

> these material conditions are insufficient, and have somehow to be supplemented. We must assume . . . an infinitely improbable accident, . . . the case is even worse—for the laws by whose blind operation this infinitely improbable

35. Ibid.

36. Ibid.

37. Ibid., 33–34.

> accident has been brought about are, by hypothesis, mechanical; and, though mechanical laws can account for rearrangements, they cannot account for creation; since, therefore, consciousness is more than rearrangement, its causes must be more than mechanical.[38]

He concluded "that the common-sense 'argument from design' . . . carries us beyond mechanical materialism, it . . . is inconsistent with Naturalism: it is inconsistent with Agnosticism. . . . The universe, or part of it, showed marks of intelligent purpose."[39] That Lewis listed this book as one of the most important he has ever read indicates that he agreed with Balfour's basic arguments as reviewed above.

In Lewis's 1946 book, *That Hideous Strength*, a Florida Edwardian mansion called Belbury was acquired by "a group of corrupt scientists seeking to remake the human race by purging it of the traditional values of freedom and dignity."[40] The people at Belbury justified this goal by "the fact that it is occurring, and it ought to be increased because of an increase taking place."[41] "Of course, the logical extension of this idea means the loss of all traditional values: murder, cruelty, theft, violation of rights are 'justified' because they are happening."[42]

Another example from *The Problem of Pain* shows that generally speaking, Lewis had little respect for Enlightenment propaganda. Specifically, Lewis noted that it would be a mistake to believe

> that our ancestors were ignorant and therefore entertained pleasing illusions about nature which the progress of science has since dispelled. For centuries, during which all men believed, the nightmare size and emptiness of the universe was already known. You will read in some books that the men of the Middle Ages thought

38. Ibid.
39. Ibid., 34.
40. Duriez, *A–Z of C. S. Lewis*, 220.
41. Williams, *Mere Humanity*, 89.
42. Crowell, "Theme of the Harmful Effects of Science," 65.

the Earth flat and the stars near, but that is a lie. Ptolemy had told them that the Earth was a mathematical point without size in relation to the distance of the fixed stars, a distance which one mediaeval popular text estimates as a hundred and seventeen million miles.[43]

43. Lewis, *Problem of Pain*, 125.

7

The Argument for Darwinism from Evil

One argument for Darwinism that Lewis had openly rejected was the argument from poor design. In the opening chapter of *The Problem of Pain* Lewis asked if the existing universe is so horrible,

> how on earth did human beings ever come to attribute it to the activity of a wise and good Creator? Men are fools, perhaps; but hardly so foolish as that. . . . The spectacle of the universe as revealed by experience can never have been the ground of religion: it must always have been something in spite of which religion, acquired from a different source, was held.[1]

Wielenberg opines that "Lewis realizes that the design argument could never lead to a *good* Higher Power; in fact, insofar as it tells us anything about the moral attributes of the Higher Power at all, it points *away* from a good Power."[2] One example Hooper gives to support this interpretation of Wielenberg is contained in a letter that Lewis wrote in 1946:

> The early loss of my mother, great unhappiness at school, and the shadow of the last war and presently the experience of it, had given me a very pessimistic view of existence. My atheism was based on it: and it still seems to me that *far* the strongest card in our enemies' hand is the actual course of the world. . . . I still think the argument

1. Lewis, *Problem of Pain*, 3.
2. Wielenberg, *God and the Reach of Reason*, 58.

> from design the weakest possible ground for Theism, and what may be called the argument from un-design the strongest for Atheism.[3]

These concerns do not reflect negatively on the argument from design, but rather on the evil in the world (the loss of his mother, his unhappiness in school, war and similar). Attempts to disprove the argument from physical design include the putative poor design of the human eye (its retina is backwards, and it has a blind spot) and the poor design in the recurrent lingual nerve, both of which have been refuted.[4]

Lewis's evidence for the design argument is primarily the moral argument, as is obvious in his explanation of the moral argument. Specifically, Lewis believes that the best evidence of the existence of God is "moral phenomena" that proves "the existence of a Higher Power that created the universe. . . . The Higher Power issues instructions and wants us to engage in morally right conduct. . . . Then there is a good mind like Higher Power that created the universe."[5] Wielenberg, from his intensive study of Lewis, concluded that Lewis believed that every person possesses

> a supernatural capacity, reason, which enables us to have genuine knowledge. Human reason must have some source, and since it has already been established that human reason cannot have been produced by nature, it must have a supernatural source. The supernatural source turns out to be God.[6]
>
> Human minds, then, are not the only supernatural entities that exist. They do not come from nowhere. Each has come into Nature from Supernature: each has its tap-root in an eternal, self-existent, rational Being, whom we call God. . . . Human thought is . . . God-kindles.[7]

3. Lewis, *Yours, Jack*, 118.
4. Bergman and Calkins, "Why the Inverted Human Retina."
5. Wielenberg, *God and the Reach of Reason*, 63.
6. Ibid., 100.
7. Lewis, *Miracles*. From Wielenberg, *God and the Reach of Reason*, 99.

Thus, God designed humans to be moral, and Lewis's argument for God to support this view from reason is as follows:

1. If naturalism is true, then knowledge exists only if natural selection could produce a capacity for knowledge (here he means wisdom) starting with creatures with no such capacity.
2. But natural selection could not produce a capacity for knowledge starting with creatures with no such capacity.
3. So: If naturalism is true, then knowledge does not exist (from 1 and 2).
4. But knowledge does exist.
5. So: naturalism is false (from 3 and 4).
6. If knowledge exists and naturalism is false, then there is a supernatural, eternal, self-existent, rational Being that is the ultimate source of all knowledge.
7. Therefore, there is a supernatural, eternal, self-existent, rational Being that is the ultimate source of all knowledge (from 4, 5, and 6).[8]

In short, Lewis rejected evolution because he concluded "that it is 'not conceivable' that evolutionary processes could produce creatures capable of knowledge from creatures incapable of knowledge."[9] Wielenberg adds that one interpretation of this is "Lewis is claiming that he (and perhaps the reader as well—perhaps *everyone*) cannot conceive of any way in which evolutionary processes could produce beings capable of knowledge. Let us say that when something is inconceivable in this sense, it is *weakly* inconceivable."[10]

Another interpretation that Wielenberg discusses is in this example "Lewis is claiming that he can see that it is impossible for evolutionary processes to yield beings capable of knowledge"

8. Wielenberg, *God and the Reach of Reason*, 101.
9. Ibid.
10. Ibid., 101–2.

because "when something is inconceivable in this sense, it is *strongly* inconceivable."[11] An example is: the concept of a round square

> is inconceivable, not merely in that I cannot conceive of a process that would produce such a shape (although that is true), but also in that I can see in a rather direct way that no such shape could exist. . . . When Lewis claims that the production of beings capable of knowledge by way of evolutionary processes is inconceivable, does he mean to say that it is weakly inconceivable or strongly inconceivable? . . . It seems, therefore, that Lewis must be claiming that he can see that the production of beings capable of knowledge by evolutionary processes is impossible. What support does Lewis offer for such a claim?[12]

Wielenberg concludes the major problem that Lewis had with the belief

> that knowledge could arise via evolutionary processes is that he thinks it is impossible that intentional mental states could be created by evolutionary processes. Nature alone cannot produce intentionality; for this, you need something outside of nature, something that Lewis calls "reason." Without supernatural reason, there would be no thinkers capable of thinking *about* the natural universe.[13]

To document this, he quotes Lewis who notes that acts

> of reasoning are not interlocked with the total interlocking system of Nature as all its other items are interlocked with one another. They are connected with it in a different way; as the understanding of a machine is certainly connected with the machine but not in the way the parts of the machine are connected with each other. The knowledge of a thing is not one of the thing's parts. In this sense something beyond Nature operates whenever we reason.[14]

11. Ibid.
12. Ibid.
13. Ibid., 103–4.
14. Ibid.

Lewis here presents a complicated and challenging argument. The weakness of the argument includes "the fact that evolutionary forces couldn't accomplish the task *in that particular way*, it does not follow that they couldn't accomplish it *at all*."[15] Nonetheless, despite

> this weakness, the argument highlights a real puzzle for naturalism, and drawing attention to this puzzle is among Lewis's most important contributions to contemporary philosophy. By Lewis's own account, doubt about the compatibility of naturalism and knowledge was one of the main intellectual components of his abandonment of naturalism and eventual conversion to Christianity. Lewis credits his friend Owen Barfield with drawing his attention to the difficulty.[16]

This line of reasoning has impressed many scholars, including the Notre Dame philosopher Alvin Plantinga. Plantinga "proposed a much-discussed argument that owes much to Lewis's argument in Miracles."[17] The other side is, in *Mere Christianity*, Lewis reasons that if we were forced

> to base our knowledge about God's nature exclusively on what we know of the observable physical universe, "we should have to conclude that He was a great artist (for the universe is a very beautiful place), but also that He is quite merciless and no friend to man (for the universe is a very dangerous and terrifying place.)"[18]

The latter is actually not an argument from classical design but, rather, as noted above, from the evil existing in the world, a fact that cannot be debated. The agnostic Bertrand Russell himself "never wavered in his endorsement of the thesis that arguments from design cannot by themselves establish the existence of the traditional God of Christianity."[19] Rather, like both

15. Ibid., 104.
16. Ibid.
17. Ibid., 105.
18. Ibid., 181–82.
19. Ibid., 183.

> Hume and Lewis, Russell saw evil in the universe as one of the major stumbling blocks for such arguments. Many have pointed to Darwin's theory of evolution as putting a dagger through the heart of the argument from design, and in some places Russell endorses this view.[20]

C. S. Lewis, though, had much to say on this controversy. First we will look at Lewis's views on theistic evolution.

20. Ibid.

8

Lewis Rejects the Theistic Evolutionist Henri Bergson

As Lewis continued his research, he increasingly even found theistic evolution problematic. An example is Henri Bergson's (1859–1914) creative evolution theory, which is a form of theistic evolution.[1] Lewis first read Bergson's book on creative evolution "as a nineteen-year-old soldier during World War I while recovering from shrapnel wounds" and felt obligated to respond to Bergson's arguments.[2]

In order to respond to Bergson, Lewis added a section to his book *Mere Christianity* that was originally based on his radio manuscript. In *Mere Christianity*, Lewis mentioned only the Materialist and Religious view, so he felt it necessary to add a discussion of theistic evolution. He called the life-force philosophy of Bergson's *Creative Evolution* "the in-between view," or "emergent evolution" (which was often termed Darwinism in this book) because he felt it was between atheism and theism. Lewis wrote in *Mere Christianity* that those who hold Bergson's view actually teach

> that the small variations by which life on this planet "evolved" from the lowest forms to Man were not due to chance but to the "striving" or "purposiveness" of a Life-Force. When people say this we must ask them whether by Life-Force they mean something with a mind. . . . If they do, then "a mind bringing life into existence and

1. Bergman, "Creative Evolution."
2. West, *Magician's Twin*, 125.

> leading it to perfection" is really a God, and their view is thus identical with the Religious. If they do not, then what is the sense in saying that something without a mind "strives" or has "purposes"? This seems to me fatal to their view. One reason why many people find Creative Evolution so attractive is that it gives one much of the emotional comfort of believing in God and none of the less pleasant consequences.[3]

Of course, the same is true of other forms of theistic evolution. Bergson was "an unsparing critic of the creative power of Darwinian natural selection,"[4] firmly believing that natural selection could not explain the existence of the natural world. Although Lewis strongly objected to Bergson's theistic evolution idea, he learned a great deal about the lethal problems of Darwinism from reading his writings. One of Lewis's most heavily annotated books was Bergson's nearly four hundred–page tome, titled in English *Creative Evolution*, that critiqued the creative ability of Darwinian natural selection theory.

Lewis wrote many notes in Bergson's book, and also underlined an even larger number of passages, later stating that the book's "critique of orthodox Darwinism" was very effective and that it "is not easy to answer."[5] Lewis concluded that the "Darwinian idea of adaptation by automatic elimination of the unadapted is a simple and clear idea" because it attributes the cause to the environment outside of the organism, namely by natural selection, which controls evolution. The problem Lewis saw with this idea is natural selection is a negative influence, not a positive influence, that

> has "great difficulty in accounting for the progressive and, so to say, rectilinear development of complex apparatus" like the vertebrate eye. Bergson stressed that Darwinism's reliance on accidental variation as the raw material for evolution made the development of highly coordinated and complex features found in biology

3. Lewis, *Mere Christianity*, 335.
4. West, *Magician's Twin*, 125.
5. Lewis, *Weight of Glory*, 89.

> nothing short of incredible. This was the case regardless of whether the accidental variations were slight or large.[6]

Bergson also noted the Darwinians argued that the mutations which occur in life that Darwinists postulate are the source of variation that natural selection selects from must have had very minor effects so as not to hinder the survival of the organism:

> For a difference which arises accidentally at one point of the visual apparatus, if it be very slight, will not hinder the functioning of the organ; and hence this first accidental variation can, in a sense, wait for complementary variations to accumulate and raise vision to a higher degree of perfection.[7]

Bergson observed that the many problems this incorrect assumption of Darwinism raised include, while

> the insensible variation does not hinder the functioning of the eye, neither does it help it, so long as the variations that are complementary do not occur. How, in that case, can the variation be retained by natural selection? Unwittingly one will reason as if the slight variation were a toothing stone set up by the organism and reserved for a later construction."[8]

Bergson noted that the mutation hypothesis is obviously of little comfort for Darwinism "which emphasizes that natural selection acts mechanically and without foresight."[9] Darwinists dealt with this problem by claiming "evolution relied on large accidental variations that provided evolutionary leaps."[10] This assumption creates "another problem, no less formidable" for Darwinism because, as Bergson asked, echoing the concept of irreducible complexity,

> How do all the parts of the visual apparatus, suddenly changed, remain so well coordinated that the eye

6. West, *Magician's Twin*, 125.
7. Ibid., 126.
8. Bergson, *Creative Evolution*, 72.
9. West, *Magician's Twin*, 125.
10. Ibid.

> continues to exercise its function? For the change of one part alone will make vision impossible, unless this change is absolutely infinitesimal. The parts must all change at once, each consulting the others.[11]

Bergson added that

> supposing chance to have granted this favor once, can we admit that it repeats the self-same favor in the course of the history of a species, so as to give rise, every time, all at once, to new complications marvelously regulated with reference to each other, and so related to former complications as to go further on in the same direction?[12]

In short, Bergson recognized that the "sheer improbability of the Darwinian explanation increases exponentially once one realizes how frequently the same complex biological features are supposed to have arisen independently in different evolutionary lineages."[13]

In Bergson's words, "What likelihood is there that, by two entirely different series of accidents being added together, two entirely different evolutions will arrive at similar results?" as we see in the claim of evolutionists called convergent evolution. The idea of evolution, Bergson concluded, was incredible because an "accidental variation, however minute," requires many

> small physical and chemical causes. An accumulation of accidental variations, such as would be necessary to produce a complex structure, requires therefore the concurrence of an almost infinite number of infinitesimal causes. Why should these causes, entirely accidental, recur the same, and in the same order, at different points of space and time?[14]

Bergson's answer to his own question was that no informed intelligent person could accept this theory of evolution "and the Darwinian himself will probably merely maintain that identical effects

11. Bergson, *Creative Evolution*, 72–73.
12. Ibid.
13. West, *Magician's Twin*, 126.
14. Bergson, *Creative Evolution*, 74.

may arise from different causes, that more than one road leads to the same spot" adding we shall not

> be fooled by a metaphor. The place reached does not give the form of the road that leads there; while an organic structure is just the accumulation of those small differences which evolution has had to go through in order to achieve it.[15]

Consequently, the "struggle for life and natural selection can be of no use to us in solving this part of the problem, for we are not concerned here with what has perished, . . . only with what has survived." From the "extensive annotations Lewis made in his personal copy of *L'Evolution Creatice*, it is clear that he understood and greatly appreciated Bergson's critique of" Darwinism.[16] West writes that, furthermore

> Lewis aptly summarized the Darwinian mechanism of adaptation according to Bergson as the "[e]limination of the unfit" and noted that it "plainly cannot account for complicated similarities on divergent lines of evolution." Lewis also noted Bergson's view that "pure Darwinism has to lean on a marvelous series of accidents" and how Darwinists try to "escape" this truth "by a bad metaphor." Lewis paid particular attention to Bergson's critique of Darwinian accounts of eye evolution in mollusks and vertebrates, concluding that "[n]atural selection . . . fails to explain these eyes."[17]

15. Ibid.

16. West, *Magician's Twin*, 127.

17. Ibid.

9

Lewis Opposes the Theistic Evolution Theory of de Chardin

A FEW YEARS AFTER he read Bergson, on August 14, 1925, Lewis wrote a letter to his father saying that the evolutionary ideas of Charles Darwin and Social Darwinist Herbert Spencer were both built "on a foundation of sand." Of note is the fact that Lewis was, as far as is known, still an atheist when he expressed these early doubts about Darwin.

Many years later, on March 5, 1960, he wrote that Jesuit priest Pierre Teilhard de Chardin's mystical theistic evolution theory "which is being praised to the skies . . . is evolution run mad."[1] Lewis also opined that the "Jesuits were quite right in forbidding him [Teilhard] to publish any more books on the subject" of his brand of theistic evolution, adding that this "prohibition probably explains the success of de Chardin among scientists."[2]

Lewis even wrote to a friend of his, Father Frederick Joseph Adelmann, on September 21, 1960, opining that the Catholic Church was "right . . . to shut up de Chardin" adding that he (Lewis) was concerned about the "enormous boosts now being given to all that Bergsonian—Shavion—pantheistic—bioidolatrous waffles";[3] bioidolatrous referred to evolution worship.

1. Lewis, *Collected Letters*, 3:1137; Ferngren and Numbers, "C. S. Lewis on Creation and Evolution," 30.

2. Lewis, *Collected Letters*, 3:1137.

3. Ibid., 1186.

Lewis Opposes the Theory of de Chardin

Father Adelmann earned his PhD from St. Louis University and chaired the philosophy department at Boston College. Although Lewis attacked Teilhard's mystical theistic evolutionism as recounted in Teilhard's book *The Phenomenon of Man*,[4] and not theistic evolution per se, his criticism nonetheless applies to other attempts to support theistic evolution.

Lewis regarded Teilhard's theistic evolution as "a unique theory of theistic evolution," a "spiritualized version of evolutionary development," where Christ is the initiator, the energizer, and the final end of the cosmic evolutionary process. Nonetheless, it was a theistic evolution theory not much different from that taught by many modern theistic evolutionists.[5]

One of Lewis's major reasons for opposing Pierre Teilhard de Chardin's theistic evolution was because it was largely only "a restatement of Bergson"[6] whom, as documented above, he also opposed. Lewis explains the reasons why Bergson's theistic evolution theory was very attractive to many persons include the fact that it had none of the negative consequences of Christian theism. Lewis wrote that when one is feeling well "you do not want to believe that the whole universe is a mere mechanical dance of atoms, it is nice to be able to think of this great mysterious Force rolling on through the centuries and carrying you on its crest."[7] Conversely, if

> you want to do something rather shabby, the Life-Force, being only a blind force, with no morals and no mind, will never interfere with you like that troublesome God we learned about when we were children. The Life-Force is a sort of tame God. You can switch it on when you want, but it will not bother you. All the thrills of religion and none of the cost. Is the Life-Force the greatest achievement of wishful thinking the world has yet seen?[8]

4. Lewis, *God in the Dock*, 523.
5. Lewis, *Collected Works.*
6. Lewis, *Collected Letters*, 3:1257.
7. Lewis, *Mere Christianity*, 34–35.
8. Ibid.

The conclusion that Lewis was very opposed to theistic evolution is also supported by his statement that it "is not Christianity which need fear the giant universe," rather, it is those belief systems that attempt to explain the "whole meaning of existence" by

> biological or social evolution on our own planet. It is the creative evolutionist, the Bergsonian or Shavian . . . who should tremble when he looks up at the night sky. For he really is committed to a sinking ship . . . attempting to ignore the discovered nature of things, as though by concentrating on the possibly upward trend in a single planet he could make himself forget the inevitable downward trend in the universe as a whole, the trend to low temperatures and irrevocable disorganization. For entropy is the real cosmic wave, and evolution only a momentary tellurian ripple within it.[9]

Furthermore, Lewis regarded the question of the origins of both life and the universe as critically important. As evidence of this, he noted that "since men were able to think, they have been wondering" how our universe and life began.[10] He then explained that two main views have existed about origins, first

> there is what is called the materialist view. People who take that view think that matter and space just happen to exist, and always have existed, nobody knows why; and that the matter, behaving in certain fixed ways, has just happened, by a sort of fluke, to produce creatures like ourselves who are able to think.[11]

Lewis was obviously very unimpressed with this view, called naturalism today, explaining in harmony with the intelligent design view that the probability is less than one in a thousand that something could have collided with the sun, causing it to

> produce the planets; and by another thousandth chance the chemicals necessary for life, and the right

9. Lewis, *God in the Dock*, 44.

10. Lewis, *Mere Christianity*, 31.

11. Ibid.

> temperature, occurred on one of these planets, and so some of the matter on this earth came alive; and then, by a very long series of chances, the living creatures developed into things like us.[12]

Lewis explained that the intelligent design view is far more reasonable because "what is behind the universe is more like a mind than it is like anything else we know . . . it is conscious, and has purposes, and prefers one thing to another . . . it made the universe . . . to produce creatures like itself . . . to the extent of having minds."[13]

Lewis then attacked the view that creationism was superseded by the modern, "scientific" view, namely evolution. He added that he did not agree with the scientists who concluded evolution replaced the creation view that has been held since Old Testament times. One reason Lewis gave as to why the creation view has been, and still is, accepted by many scientists is the fact that "wherever there have been thinking men both views [creation and evolution] turn up."[14]

Last, Lewis stressed that all too often science has become a religion, and one cannot determine which view, creation or evolution, is the correct view of origins by science alone because science only

> works by experiments. It watches how things behave. Every scientific statement in the long run, however complicated it looks, really means something like . . . "I put some of this stuff in a pot and heated it to such-and-such a temperature and it did so-and-so."[15]

He then stressed that he is not degrading science in general, but rather he is only saying what the job of science is, adding "the more scientific a man is, the more [I believe] he would agree with me that this is the job of science—and a very useful and necessary job it is. . . . But why anything comes to be . . . and whether there is

12. Ibid., 32.
13. Ibid.
14. Ibid.
15. Ibid.

anything behind the things science observes . . . is not a scientific question."[16]

Lewis concluded that the origins of life problem is not a question that the scientific method can answer, because, if there is "Something Behind" the creation, "then either it will have to remain altogether unknown to men or else make itself known in some different way. . . . And real scientists do not usually make [claims about theology]. . . . It is usually the journalists and popular novelists who have picked up a few odds and ends of half-baked science from textbooks who [do]."[17]

In other words, Lewis did not have a problem with the results of the empirical research supporting microevolution, a process that creationists refer to as variation within the Genesis kinds. Modern examples of this work of scientists that explore the variation within the Genesis kinds includes research on bacterial resistance, the peppered moth, variation of Darwin's finch beaks and similar. In his later writing, Lewis detailed in more depth his concern about both macroevolution and naturalism.

Lewis repeatedly stressed that science has its place, but has clear limits, writing: "Let scientists tell us about sciences. But government involves questions about the good for man, and justice, and what things are worth having at what price; and on these [things] scientific training gives a man's opinion no added value."[18] Canadian journalist Denyse O'Leary concluded from her study of Lewis that he was

> careful to distinguish between evolution as a theory in biology and Evolution as an idea that came to dominate the politics and religion of his time. He noted that decades before Darwin's *On the Origin of Species*, poets and musicians had started proclaiming that humanity was inevitably evolving, onward and upward, to a glorious

16. Ibid.
17. Ibid.
18. Lewis, *God in the Dock*, 315.

> future, "I grew up believing in this Myth and I have felt—I still feel—its almost perfect grandeur," he wrote.[19]

She added that Lewis believed that a big difference existed

> between the myth of Evolution preached by poets and the theory in biology. Lewis made quite clear to his readers that the biological theory of Darwinism does not argue that there will be inevitable, continuous *improvements* over time. It only explains continuous *change* over time. The change can be degeneration or decline. . . . As applied to human society, the myth of evolution morphed from a *theory* about changes to a supposed *fact* about improvements. It became a powerful weapon for good or ill in the hands of social reformers and politicians.[20]

O'Leary here refers to the problem of entropy for evolution.[21] In his "Funeral of a Great Myth," Lewis wrote that to persons who were "brought up on the Myth nothing seems more normal, more natural, more plausible, than that chaos should turn into order, death into life, ignorance into knowledge."[22] O'Leary adds that Lewis believed "continuous improvement without human effort seemed so plausible" to Darwinists

> that contrary examples in nature were simply ignored. For example popular presentations of evolution typically feature the evolution of the modern horse from a bulgy little pawed creature. They do not highlight the evolution of an active, independent creature into a degenerate, disease-causing parasite, though that happens, too.[23]

Lewis also had some sharp comments to make about the realities of science. In *The Pilgrim's Regress*—which follows the progress of a fictional character through the philosophical landscape, including

19. O'Leary, *By Design or by Chance?*, 63.

20. Ibid., 63–64.

21. See Lewis, *God in the Dock*, 44.

22. O'Leary, *By Design or by Chance?*, 112. Lewis wrote: "I grew up believing in this Myth and I have felt—I still feel—its almost perfect grandeur (Lewis, *Christian Reflections*, 110).

23. O'Leary, *By Design or by Chance?*, 112.

nihilism, before eventually arriving at traditional Christianity—Lewis wrote that the character in his book, as is true of so many persons today, had "a very crude notion of how science actually works. To put it simply" a hypothesis

> establishes itself by a cumulative process: or, to use popular language, *if you make the same guess often enough it ceases to be a guess and becomes a Scientific Fact.*
>
> After he had thought for a while, John said: "I think I see. Most of the stories about the Landlord are probably untrue; therefore the rest are probably untrue."
>
> "Well, that is as near as a beginner can get to it. . . . But when you have had . . . scientific training you will find that you can be quite certain about all sorts of things which now seem to you only probable."[24]

24. Lewis, *Pilgrim's Regress*, 28, emphasis added.

10

Lewis Teaches a Creation Worldview

Lewis repeatedly not only criticized evolution, but taught a creation worldview. In his various writings, such as in the book *The Magician's Nephew*, one of the *Chronicles of Narnia*, the creation of Narnia is described in ways that have some parallel to the biblical creation account. He also wrote that the reason the church exists is to draw men to Christ and if

> they are not doing that, all the cathedrals, clergy, missions, sermons, even the Bible itself, are simply a waste of time. God became Man for no other purpose. It is even doubtful . . . whether the whole universe was created for any other purpose. It says in the Bible that the whole universe was made for Christ. . . . We do not know what (if anything) lives in the parts of it that are millions of miles away from this Earth. Even on this Earth we do not know how it applies to things other than men. . . . We have been shown the plan only in so far as it concerns ourselves.[1]

He even wondered, if nature, which he defines as actually only "space and time and matter," could create a situation to create everything in existence. For example, is there

> no other way of getting many eternal spirits except by first making many natural creatures, in a universe, and then spiritualizing them? . . . The idea that the whole human race is, in a sense, one thing—one huge organism, like a tree—must not be confused with the idea that individual differences do not matter or that real people, Tom

1. Lewis, *Mere Christianity*, 171.

> and Nobby and Kate, are somehow less important than collective things like classes, races, and so forth. Indeed the two ideas are opposites.[2]

Lewis believed that God, through Christ "created the whole universe, became not only a man but [before that] a baby, and before that a *fœtus* inside a Woman's body. If you want to get the hang of it, think how you would like to become a slug or a crab."[3] Furthermore, he wrote Christianity teaches that God not only made the world, but also created

> space and time, heat and cold, and all the colours and tastes, and all the animals and vegetables, . . . things that God "made up out of His head" as a man makes up a story. But . . . [the atheists] also think that a great many things have gone wrong with the world that God made and that God insists, and insists very loudly, on our putting them right again.[4]

This reasoning raises a major question, namely if

> a good God made the world why has it gone wrong? And for many years I simply refused to listen to the Christian answers to this question, because I kept on feeling . . . however clever your arguments are, isn't it much simpler and easier to say that the world was not made by any intelligent power? Aren't all your arguments simply a complicated attempt to avoid the obvious?[5]

Of course, to Lewis the obvious answer is a good God made the world. Lewis also objected to Einstein's god because Lewis's picture of God was the personal, Creator God as taught by the Judeo-Christian tradition. He rejected the mechanism of emergent evolution, today often called atheistic evolution or macroevolution, because, like all materialistic systems, it

> breaks down at the problem of knowledge. If thought is the . . . irrelevant product of cerebral motions, what

2. Ibid.
3. Ibid., 156.
4. Ibid., 45.
5. Ibid.

> reason have we to trust it? As for emergent evolution, if anyone insists on using the word *God* to mean "whatever the universe happens to be going to do next," of course we cannot prevent him. But nobody would in fact so use it unless he had a secret belief that what is coming next will be an improvement [which is emergent evolution].[6]

He added that this belief is not only unwarranted, but

> presents peculiar difficulties to an emergent evolutionist. If things can improve, this means that there must be some absolute standard of good above and outside the cosmic process to which that process can approximate. There is no sense in talking of "becoming better" if better means simply "what we are becoming"—it is like congratulating yourself on reaching your destination and defining destination as "the place you have reached." Mellontolatry, or the worship of the future, is a *fuddled* religion.[7]

Lewis has also thought about the implications of creationism, writing that

> God, besides being the Great Creator, is the Tragic Redeemer. Perhaps the Tragic Creator too. For I am not sure that the great canyon of anguish which lies across our lives is *solely* due to some prehistoric catastrophe. Something tragic may . . . be inherent in the very act of creation.[8]

Lewis also accepted Creation *ex nihilo*; adding that when he speaks of God "uttering" or "inventing" creatures, he is not "watering down the concept of creation" but rather is

> trying to give it, by remote analogies, some sort of content. I know that to create is defined as "to make out of nothing," *ex nihilo* . . . "*not* out of any pre-existing material." It can't mean that God makes what God has not thought of or that He gives His creatures any powers or beauties which He Himself does not possess. Why, we think that even human work comes nearest to creation

6. Lewis, *God in the Dock*, 21.

7. Ibid.

8. Lewis, *Letters to Malcolm*, 91.

> when the maker has "got it all out of his own head." . . . This act, as it is for God, must always remain totally inconceivable to man. For we—never, in the ultimate sense, *make*. We only build. We always have materials to build from. All we can know about the act of creation must be derived from what we can gather about the relation of the creatures to their Creator.[9]

In other words, "Creation" as applied to human authorship is a misleading term; humans can only rearrange the elements that God has created. Only God can create *ex nihilo*.

Evolution as Mental or Spiritual Growth

Lewis often used the term "evolution" to refer to mental or spiritual growth, which created problems when he used this term in other contexts. For example, with "shrewd insight into the modern mind" Lewis turned "to evolution in order to explain what Christianity is all about. The 'new men' are presented as the next stage in evolution—or rather, as the stage that part of humanity has already reached."[10] Another example is in his inaugural lecture at Cambridge in 1954, as noted above, Lewis proposed

> that the largest shift in human culture was not, as usually claimed, the shift from Medieval to Renaissance but rather that which occurred early in the nineteenth century and introduced the post-Christian era. He expressed the surprising idea that Christians and ancient pagans had much more in common than either has with the post-Christian culture of today, and he enumerated four main areas in which the change could be observed: politics, the arts, religion, and "the birth of machines."[11]

This shift, Lewis concluded, facilitated the nineteenth-century belief in what he called spontaneous progress that "in turn owes something to Darwin's theory of evolution and perhaps to the 'myth

9. Ibid., 72–73.

10. Walsh, *C. S. Lewis*, 28.

11. The speech was quoted in Kilby, *Christian World of C. S. Lewis*, 174.

of universal evolutionism,' which is different from Darwin and also pre-dates him."[12] When discussing "the Darwinian hypothesis . . . he [Lewis] always makes a clear distinction between men and animals."[13] Conversely he defines "universal evolutionism,"

> as "the belief that the very formula of universal process is from imperfect to perfect, from small beginnings to great endings, from the rudimentary to the elaborate: the belief which makes people find it natural to think that morality springs from savage taboos, adult sentiment from infantile sexual maladjustments, thought from instinct, mind from matter, organic from inorganic, cosmos from chaos." Though he believes this to be the very image of contemporary thought, he regards it as "immensely unplausible because it makes the general course of nature so very unlike those parts of nature we can observe." We would do better, he says, to emphasize less that an adult human being came from an embryo than that the embryo was produced by two adult human beings.[14]

From this description it is clear that the worldview Lewis opposes is clearly orthodox Darwinism. The Christian view is

> precisely that the Next Step has already appeared. And it is really new. It isn't a change from brainy men to brainier men: it is a change that goes off in a totally different direction—a change from being the creatures of God to being sons of God. The first instance appeared in Palestine two thousand years ago.[15]

The final pages of Lewis's book emphasize the price of becoming a Christian: "But there must be a real giving up of the self. You must throw it away 'blindly' so to speak. Christ will in fact give you a real personality."[16]

12. Kilby, *Christian World of C. S. Lewis*, 174.
13. Ibid.
14. Ibid., 174–75.
15. Walsh, *C. S. Lewis*, 28.
16. Ibid.

11

Statements That Indicate Lewis Was a Theistic Evolutionist

ALTHOUGH A FEW STATEMENTS that Lewis made may indicate he was a theistic evolutionist, when examined in context, and in view of the stage of his intellectual and spiritual growth, the statements do not openly support this conclusion. An example of what claims to be a "comprehensive study" of Lewis's views on intelligent design and evolution, theology professor Michael L. Peterson quoted Lewis in his edited version of what Lewis wrote in *Mere Christianity*[1] as saying, "Perhaps a modern man can understand the Christian idea [of transformation] best if he takes it in connection with Evolution. Everyone now knows . . . that man has evolved from lower types of life."[2]

As Wile notes: "This quote makes it sound like Lewis firmly believed that man evolved from lower life forms such as apes. However, that's not what Lewis wrote."[3] The entire quote, with the sections that Peterson lifted in bold, is as follows:

> Perhaps a modern man can understand the Christian idea best if he takes it in connection with Evolution. Everyone now knows about Evolution (though, of course, some educated people disbelieve it): everyone has been told that man has evolved from lower types of life.[4]

1 Peterson, "C. S. Lewis on Evolution," 264.

2. Ibid.

3. Wile, "Everyone Wants a Piece of C. S. Lewis."

4. Ibid.

As Wile notes, this

> passage says something quite different from what Peterson wants you to believe. It doesn't at all imply that Lewis believes man evolved from lower types of life. It doesn't even imply that Lewis thinks everyone else does. In fact, he specifically says that he knows there are some educated people who don't believe in it. So Lewis was making a much more tentative statement about man evolving from lower forms of life than what Peterson wants you to think he was making. It is unfortunate that Peterson quotes Lewis out of context, simply to make it look like Lewis agrees with him.[5]

The sentence in its entirety clearly shows that, far from asserting "Evolution" is something that "everyone now knows," Lewis was stating only that "everyone now knows *about* Evolution," and "everyone has been *told*" about it. He here was describing the popular view, not claiming that human evolution is true. Lest someone misunderstand that Lewis was endorsing the view of evolution that "everyone has been told" Lewis added the caveat, "of course, some educated people disbelieve it."[6]

Lewis and the Genesis Fall

In a study of the Adam-Eve doctrine, Collins wrote that Lewis is vague in his book *The Problem of Pain* on a literal Adam and Eve, which he (Lewis) calls an "imaginative exercise," but "in his other books, he [Lewis] keeps to a particular Adam and Eve, as he has great respect for the form of the story in Genesis." An example is in the sequel to the *Silent Planet*, humans were still innocent and thus were at the Adam and Eve stage.[7] Collins also observed that Lewis's imaginative exercise has "moved us away from the Biblical Story," but, nonetheless, he

5. Ibid., 1.
6. West, *Magician's Twin*, 112.
7. Dickerson and O'Hara, *Narnia and the Fields of Arbol*, 186.

> preserves the *historical character of the fall*: that is, it is an event—or cluster of events—that actually took place, and changed human life forever. This certainly sets his view apart from all views that see sin as the result of something "timeless and eternal" and thus nonhistorical (as in Karl Barth), or as something inherent in God's creation (as in many modern theologians).[8]

Collins also noted that the major difficulty he had

> with Lewis's view lies in his clause, "We do not know *how many* of these creatures God made." He is not asserting that there *must* have been more than Adam and Eve; he is declaring the question immaterial to the discussion. If, however, we take our cue from Lewis's own mention of solidarity and "in Adam," . . . then we have a way of pushing Lewis's scenario into a more acceptable direction. That is we should make it more like . . . Adam as the chieftain and Eve as his queen.[9]

Lewis himself also wrote in *The Problem of Pain* that even the details of the fall may be literal: "For all I can see it might have concerned the literal eating of a fruit."[10]

Another example where Lewis discusses the Genesis fall is also in *The Problem of Pain*, which was the first of a series of popular works that Lewis wrote on Christian doctrine. This book was authored in 1940, not long after Lewis converted to Christianity from agnosticism when he was evidently still somewhat ambivalent on the subject of evolution. In this book, Lewis considered the problem of suffering from a purely theoretical standpoint, which he argued was valid *even if* theistic evolution were true.

When arguing specifically for the orthodox Genesis fall-of-man doctrine, Lewis made it clear that the account requires accepting a sinless perfect Adam, or at least a man that was a fully human species, and a fall from grace. Why then did Lewis write

8. Collins, *Did Adam and Eve Really Exist?*, 130, emphasis added.

9. Ibid.

10. Lewis, *Problem of Pain*, 76, quoted in Kilby, *Christian World of C. S. Lewis*, 154.

"if by claiming that man rose from brutality you mean simply that man is physically from animals, I have no objection?"[11]

He also did *not* say he agreed with this view, but that he had "no objection," if people wanted to believe this view, evidently because Lewis here was arguing that the doctrine of the Genesis fall could be defended, *even* if one tried to argue "that man physically descended from the animals." Likely one reason is because even this view still allows for the acceptance of the fall.

Brute and savage man refers to something very different than what is meant by the fall. One interpretation of the fall into sin, as revealed in the Scriptures, involves not brute bodies, but cruel, treacherous, ferocious, and evil behavior, not simply a fall from a less complex or less industrial society as evolutionists believe existed in the so-called primitive societies.[12] Roberts noted that "the literal reality of Lewis's mythical figures (the Savior/Fisher King, the Devil, Adam and Eve) is only possible via Lewis's conservative Christian faith."[13] In a letter to a Miss Breckenridge dated August 1, 1949, Lewis wrote that there

> is *no* relation of any importance between the Fall and Evolution. The doctrine of Evolution is that organisms have changed, sometimes for what we call (biologically) the better . . . quite often for what we call (biologically) the worse. . . . The doctrine of the Fall is that at one particular point one species, Man, tumbled down a moral cliff. There is neither opposition nor support between the two doctrines. . . . Evolution is not only not a doctrine of moral improvements, but of biological changes, some improvements, some deteriorations.[14]

Lewis's definition of evolution is hardly the orthodox view, which postulates an evolution from simple organic compounds to modern humans. In another article, even though he made his objections to Darwinism perfectly clear, Lewis wrote "*for the purpose of*

11. Ibid., 60.

12. Ibid., 61.

13. Roberts, *Silk and Potatoes*, 23.

14. Lewis, *Collected Letters*, 2:962, emphasis added.

this article I am assuming that Darwinian biology is correct," again attempting to show that this particular argument was still valid, even if Darwinian evolution was true.

Lewis uses the same reasoning in the passage that Peterson selectively quoted to prove that he (Lewis) was a theistic evolutionist, or even a Darwinist. The passage is as follows, with the parts that Peterson selected in italics.[15] This passage was also first published in 1940, not long after Lewis's conversion from atheism:

> *For long centuries God perfected the animal form which was to become the vehicle of humanity and the image of Himself.* He [God] gave it hands whose thumb could be applied to each of the fingers, and jaws and teeth and throat capable of articulation, and a brain sufficiently complex to execute all the material motions whereby rational thought is incarnated. *The creature may have existed for ages in this state before it became man*: it may even have been clever enough to make things which a modern archaeologist would accept as proof of its humanity. But it was only an animal because all its physical and psychical processes were directed to purely material and natural ends. Then, *in the fullness of time, God caused to descend upon this organism*, both on its psychology and physiology, *a new kind of consciousness which could say "I" and "me,"* which could look upon itself as an object, *which knew God*, which *could make judgments of truth, beauty, and goodness*, and which was so far above time that it could perceive time flowing past. . . . Man was then all consciousness.[16]

This passage is again hypothetical, a story that refers to human mental and spiritual growth. This interpretation is consistent with what Lewis wrote in his "Funeral of a Great Myth" essay,[17] where Lewis makes it clear that he is willing to accept microevolution, but is not willing to accept macroevolution, such as the

15. Peterson, "C. S. Lewis on Evolution," 260.

16. Lewis, *Problem of Pain*, 77, emphasis added to show the section Peterson quoted.

17. Lewis, *Christian Reflections*, 85.

evolution of all higher forms of life from single-celled animals, writing, in *Christian Reflections* that

> for the scientist Evolution is purely a biological theorem. It takes over organic life on this planet as a going concern and tries to explain certain changes within that field. It makes no cosmic statements, no metaphysical statements, no eschatological statements. Granted that we now have minds we can trust, granted that organic life came to exist, it tries to explain, say, how a species that once had wings came to lose them. It explains this by the negative effect of environment operating on small variations. It does not in itself explain the origin of organic life, nor of the variations, nor does it discuss the origin and validity of reason. *It may well tell you how the brain, through which reason now operates, arose*, but that is a different matter.[18]

Peterson uses this quote to claim that, "clearly, Lewis accepts the Darwinian concept of 'common descent with modification.'"[19] The full quote and the context of the chapter also shed a very different light on Lewis's words than Peterson implied. Lewis *prefaced* the above quote by stressing, "What exactly happened when Man fell, we do not know, but *if it is legitimate to guess*, I offer the following picture—a 'myth' in the Socratic sense, a not unlikely tale."[20] One interpretation of a myth in the Socratic sense is a "story that *may have been* historical fact."[21]

The word myth, as used in this context, was explained by Edmund Fuller, who opined "that Lewis's science-fiction trilogy represented a fresh telling of the Christian myth of the fall of man. So used, myth does not mean fiction, of course, but truth through symbolism."[22] Fuller added that Lewis

18. Lewis, *Christian Reflections*, 107, emphasis added.
19. Peterson, "C. S. Lewis on Evolution," 260.
20. Lewis, *Problem of Pain*, 76.
21. Collins, *Did Adam and Eve Really Exist?*, 128.
22. White, *Image of Man*, 128.

> dramatizes and clarifies for our age the Christian teaching about man's peculiar dilemma in the order of Creation. The tragic fact of man's condition is that he is other than he was intended to be; the deep springs of his will have been subverted—he cannot do consistently the good that he would, but does instead the evil that he would not do.[23]

Schmerl spoke of this science fiction trilogy as "an imaginative extension of Christian mythology, centering around a new battle between God and his angels and Satan and his devils, fought on three planets."[24]

In another letter, dated December 29, 1958, Lewis

> described his novel *Perelandra* as the working out of the "supposition" that what happened to Adam and Eve on earth, could happen to another first couple elsewhere: "Suppose, even now, in some other planet there were a first couple undergoing the same [temptation] that Adam and Eve underwent here [on earth], but successfully."[25]

Lewis even viewed the vast astronomical distance in the universe as "God's quarantine precautions" to "prevent the spiritual infection of a Fallen species from spreading" to other planets.[26]

Perelandra is the second volume of Lewis's science fiction trilogy. What is particularly significant in this volume is the garden of Eden illustration it contains, specifically the planet Perelandra (Venus) is a paradise ocean world that is depicted as an analogue of the garden of Eden story. According to Fuller, "The tempting of the first woman of Perelandra entails an extraordinarily intricate, far-reaching debate at the deepest level of moral theology."[27]

Furthermore, the rest of this chapter in *The Problem of Pain* strongly indicates that Lewis personally believed in a literal

23. Fuller, *Books with Men behind Them*, 155.
24. Schmerl, "Reason's Dream," 60.
25. Ibid., 60. The letter is from *Collected Letters*, 3:1004.
26. Deasy, "God, Space, and C. S. Lewis," 422.
27. White, *Image of Man in C. S. Lewis*, 128.

Adam.[28] For example, Lewis wrote that "the Holy Spirit would not have allowed the creation account of Adam and Eve and the fall" in the Bible, and this view would not have achieved "the assent of great [church] doctors unless it . . . was true."[29] Lewis adds that the Adam and Eve account about "the magic apple . . . brings together the trees of life and knowledge and contains a deeper and subtler truth than the version which makes the apple simply and solely a pledge of obedience."[30]

In the chapter titled "The Fall of Man" in *The Problem of Pain*, Lewis identifies Adam and Eve's original sin as wanting "to 'call their souls their own,' but that is to live a lie, for our souls are not, in fact, our own. They wanted some corner of the universe of which they could say to God 'This is our business, not yours.' But there is no such corner. They wanted to be nouns, but they were, and eternally must be, mere adjectives."[31]

In short, from a review of numerous passages, it is safe to agree with Lewis scholar and biographer Professor Colin Duriez's conclusion that Lewis "believed in a real historical fall by disobedient mankind that affected the whole of nature."[32] One reason Lewis opposed evolutionism was because "evolutionism was opposed to the doctrine of original sin."[33] Duriez defined Adam and Eve as "the first humans with all people in every part of the world descending from them."[34]

This is one reason why in Lewis's novels, such as *The Chronicles of Narnia*, the throne may be occupied only by "the sons of Adam and the daughters of Eve."[35] Lewis also believed that the fall affected the animals as well as humans.[36] In other words, Lewis

28. Lewis, *Problem of Pain*, 69–73.

29. Ibid., 72.

30. Ibid.

31. Ibid., 80.

32. Duriez, *A–Z of C. S. Lewis*, 215.

33. Dickerson and O'Hara, *Narnia and the Fields of Arbol*, 278.

34. Duriez, *A–Z of C. S. Lewis*, 15.

35. Ibid., 81.

36. Lewis, *Collected Letters*, 2:460.

often described the fall in such a way that it required not only a literal Adam, often using the pronoun "he," but also required the origin of all creation, including of life, the earth, and the plants, all which are clearly literal.

12

Evolution Cannot Explain the Origin of Life or the Mind

We argued earlier that, to be consistent, in Lewis's "Funeral of a Great Myth" essay[1] his statement, "*It may well tell you how the brain, through which reason now operates, arose*," could refer, not to the evolution of the brain from simple one-celled life, but to modern mankind's ideas compared to those of men living in primitive societies.

Note that in his writing, Lewis says evolution *cannot* explain the origin of life or the origin of the mind; thus he is clearly not an evolutionist as commonly defined. When Lewis wrote the funeral essay, he was still careful not to openly challenge the evolutionary establishment. Consequently, he wrote that it "may well tell you" rather than "the fact that." The fact is, Lewis wrote many seemingly contradictory statements that have to be interpreted in context. Even though one could take quotes from Lewis in an attempt to prove the evolutionary case, endeavoring to be consistent, one must look at all of his writings on this topic to understand the few places where Lewis *appears* to support macroevolution.

Evidence for this view includes an event documented by a person Lewis referred to as "A.N." based on an interview with his Oxford colleague, professor Helen Gardner. Lewis biographer A. N. Wilson wrote that, at a dinner party with friends, the conversation "turned on the interesting question of whom" those present would most look forward to personally meeting after death. One

1. Lewis, *Christian Reflections*, 85.

person answered Shakespeare, another St. Paul. When Lewis was asked the same question, he answered, "I have no difficulty in deciding, I want to meet Adam." He went on to explain why, very much in the terms he outlined in *A Preface to Paradise Lost*, where Lewis wrote,

> Adam was, from the first, a man in knowledge as well as in stature. He alone of all men "had been in Eden, in the garden of God, he had walked up and down in the midst of the stones of fire." He was endowed, says Athanasius, with "a vision of God so far-reaching that he could contemplate the eternity of the Divine Essence and the coming operations of His Word." He was "a heavenly being" according to St. Ambrose, who breathed the aether and was accustomed to converse with God "face to face."[2]

Wilson comments that

> Adam is not likely, if she has anything to do with it, to converse with [Oxford professor] Helen Gardner. . . . Even, she told Lewis, if there really were, historically, someone whom we could name as "the first man," he would be a Neanderthal ape-like figure, whose conversation she could not conceive of finding interesting. A stony silence fell on the dinner table. Then Lewis said gruffly, "I see we have a Darwinian in our midst." Helen Gardner was never invited again. Another Oxford woman with whom Lewis famously crossed swords at this period was Elizabeth Anscombe, the philosopher.[3]

This exchange also supports the view that Lewis believed in a literal Adam, and also was not a Darwinist.

In the book *The Problem of Pain*, the two chapters "Human Wickedness" and "The Fall of Man," Lewis opens with a statement similar to one he made in his essay "Christian Apologetics." As Bloom explains, until modern humans realize that they are sinful, "Christianity has little to say to them," and therefore Lewis attempts to convince readers of their sinfulness. The second step

2. Quoted in Wilson, *C. S. Lewis*, 210.

3. Wilson, *C. S. Lewis*, 210.

is an attempt "to establish the doctrine of Original Sin without being literalistic about Adam and Eve." To do this Lewis offers the following response: "a 'myth' in the Socratic sense, a not unlikely tale."[4] Bloom interprets this account in a very different way:

> The myth (or fabulous history) starts with the evolution of mankind as animals to which, at some point in time, god gave the gift of self-consciousness and awareness of the true, the good, and the beautiful—Lewis does not point out the Platonism in the triple awareness. The rest of the account covers the Fall—that is, an act of self-will—and then dwindles into reflections on the event.[5]

As we have seen from Lewis's own writings, he made it clear that he believed "man has fallen from the state of innocence in which he was created," and he therefore rejects "any theory which contradicts this."[6] As Professor Walsh wrote, to Lewis—as also was true of orthodox Christianity—Christ, was "the 'new Adam,' through whom humanity is to be restored to its original harmony with God. The final restoration will mean that man will once again have the same command over nature that Lewis attributes to the first men."[7]

Even if Lewis thought the Adam account was fiction, the words of Adam and Eve were, as Walsh writes, ringing in the lead characters' ears of Lewis's books.[8] He added in this letter that it was "not yet obvious that *all* theories of evolution contradict it."[9] As we will document, a few years later it became obvious to Lewis that Darwinism *does* contradict it, and greatly so. As one of Lewis's characters, Aslan, states, "We came from Lord Adam and the Lady Eve" because all humans are "Sons of Adam and Daughters of Eve."[10]

4. Bloom, *C. S. Lewis*, 118.
5. Ibid.
6. Lewis, letter dated September 23, 1944, in *Collected Letters*, 2:842.
7. Walsh, *C. S. Lewis: Apostle to the Skeptics*, 105–6.
8. Ibid., 44.
9. Lewis, letter dated September 23, 1944, in *Collected Letters*, 2:842.
10. Dickerson and O'Hara, *Narnia and the Fields of Arbol*, 65.

Using modern terminology, microevolution does not contradict the fall, but macroevolution or naturalistic evolution clearly does. Furthermore, Lewis argues that the unfallen Adam would not be inferior to us, but rather superior, because the powers of Jesus

> and the possible powers of unfallen Adam, are in rather a different category from either. Magic would be the artificial and local recovery of what Adam enjoyed normally: Which makes a difference. If Our Lord did His miracles *qua* God and not *qua* Man then the difference would be even greater.[11]

Again and again, Lewis wrote about how central the doctrine of Adam and Eve was to Christianity, which logically requires "the doctrines of the Creation and the Fall" to be true, adding that some

> hazy adumbrations of a doctrine of the Fall can be found in Paganism; but it is quite astonishing how rarely outside Christianity we find . . . a real doctrine of Creation. In Polytheism the gods are usually the product of a universe already in existence. . . . In Pantheism the universe is never something that God made. It is an emanation, something that oozes out of Him, or an appearance, something He looks like to us but really is not. . . . Polytheism is always, in the long run, nature-worship: Pantheism is always, in the long run, hostility to nature.[12]

Lewis even speculated that, if intelligent life is discovered in outer space, a problem is the "possibility that unfallen peoples may inhabit other planets."[13] In his science fiction novel *Perelandra*, Lewis's characters also discuss the fall.[14]

Lewis also treated Adam as a real historical person in his private correspondence. He once wrote to his father that "since the Fall of Adam . . . [we] are but half men."[15] He wrote to his friend, Italian priest St. Giovanni Calabria on March 17, 1953, that a "nec-

11. Lewis, *Collected Letters*, 2:842.
12. Lewis, *God in the Dock*, 149.
13. Deasy, "God, Space, and C. S. Lewis," 421.
14. Ibid., 422.
15. Lewis, *Collected Letters*, 2:979.

essary doctrine [held by both Catholics and Protestants is] that we are . . . closely joined together alike with the sinner Adam and with the Just One, Jesus."[16] And "the unity of the whole human race exists" because we are all descendents of Adam.[17]

For all of these reasons, claims such as by Joe Christopher, who dogmatically stated, "What is significant in *The Problem of Pain* is that Lewis *does not believe* the *Adam and Eve* story can be taken seriously by his audience at a *literal* level in a Darwinian age," are erroneous.[18]

Lewis also accepted creation *ex nihilo*, writing the "meaning of *creation* . . . I take . . . to mean . . . without pre-existing material (to cause both the form & matter of) *something pre-conceived in the Causer's thought.*"[19]

Thus, even in his early postconversion life, Lewis did not "clearly accept . . . the Darwinian concept of 'common descent with modification'" but, at the most, he believed that this view could be an option for a Christian. In other words, as noted above, the doctrine of the fall, which was central to the thesis in his book *The Problem of Pain*, can be explained *even if* Darwinism was true.

This is logical in view of the fact that Lewis once wrote that he writes for atheists and agnostics.[20] As he explained, "I say 'evolution as popularly imagined.' I am not in the least concerned to refute Darwinism as a theorem in biology," acknowledging that there "may be flaws in that theorem," and there

> may be signs that biologists are already contemplating a withdrawal from the whole Darwinian position, but I claim to be no judge of such signs. It can even be argued that what Darwin really accounted for was not the origin, but the elimination of species. . . . For purposes of this article I am assuming that Darwinian biology is correct. What I want to point out is the illegitimate transition

16. Lewis, *Collected Letters*, 3:306.
17. Ibid.
18. Bloom, *C. S. Lewis*, 118, emphasis added.
19. Lewis, *Collected Letters*, 2:870.
20. Lewis, *World's Last Night*, 49.

> from the Darwinian theorem in biology to the modern myth of evolutionism or developmentalism or progress in general. The first thing to notice is that the myth arose earlier than the theorem, in advance of all evidence.[21]

As noted by Crowell, Lewis used the term developmentalism to refer to Darwinian evolution, as well as for the tendency for "developmental change which we call Evolution, is justified by the fact that it is a general characteristic of biological entities."[22]

21. Ibid., 101.

22. Williams, *Mere Humanity*. 88, from Lewis, *That Hideous Strength*, 295.

13

The Fall Appears in His Novels

THE FALL DOCTRINE WAS even supported in Lewis's novels. The common notion was that inhabitants of other planets would be cruel monsters, or monsters like some of H. G. Wells's creatures in his science fiction novels. These monsters destroyed men who meant them no harm. Lewis's secretary, Walter Hooper, wrote that in Lewis's novels, fallen men went to planets where they found unfallen rational creatures. The Malacandra inhabitants did not even have words for sin or evil. They say only that some person is bent, meaning a created being who was disobedient is simply the "Bent One."[1]

Lewis recognized that just as Ptolemaic astronomy once was but is no longer accepted, some people, called theistic evolutionists, believe that "Evolution . . . is the *assumed* background of Christianity". Likewise, as Lewis studied the matter, he came to conclude that Darwinism is *not* the background of Christianity.[2]

Even if Professor Michael Peterson's interpretation of Lewis's view on evolution was valid, it must be remembered that the *Problem of Pain* was written not long after Lewis converted from atheism and that Lewis became more hostile toward Darwinism as he learned more about it. As we will document, Lewis had major problems with common descent, especially as he studied and thought about the implications of the doctrine in more detail. To lift one section from his lifelong writings and claim that "clearly . . . Lewis accepts the Darwinian concept of 'common descent'" as

1. Lewis, *Christian Reflections*, 174.
2. Lewis, *Collected Letters*, 2:953.

Peterson did, would be like concluding that Lewis, based on his early beliefs, clearly was an atheist.[3] In *Christian Reflections*, Lewis writes it is his view that to

> the biologist, Evolution is a hypothesis. It covers more of the facts than any other hypothesis at present on the market, and is therefore to be accepted unless, or until, some new supposal can be shown to cover still more facts with even fewer assumptions. At least, that is what I think most biologists would say.[4]

Of course, this view is an outsider's evaluation of what Lewis felt biologists believed, not what he (Lewis) believed. Lewis also qualified his above statement, stating he had major doubts about common descent because

> Darwinism gives no support to the belief that natural selection, working upon chance variations, has a general tendency to produce improvement. The illusion that it has comes from confining our attention to a few species which have (by some possibly arbitrary standard of our own) changed for the better. Thus the horse has improved in the sense that *protohippos* would be less useful to us than his modern descendant. . . . But a great many of the changes produced by evolution are not improvements by any conceivable standard. . . . There is no general law of progress in biological history.[5]

Lewis accepted microevolution change by evolution, but not "progress in biological history" which is what Darwinism is all about, such as eyespots evolving into vertebrate eyes by hundreds of examples of progress in biology. Lewis also wrote, "Evolution is not only not a doctrine of *moral* improvements, but of biological changes, some improvements, some deteriorations."[6] One statement that is less clear is: "The anthropoid has improved in

3. Peterson, "C. S. Lewis on Evolution," 260.
4. Lewis, *Christian Reflections*, 83.
5. Lewis, *World's Last Night*, 103.
6. Lewis, *Mere Christianity*, 218; Lewis, *Letters of C. S. Lewis*, 392–93.

the sense that he now is Ourselves."[7] By anthropoid, it appears he means a "primitive," but fully human, man, not a prehuman ape-man as Darwinism teaches. In Lewis's terms, "primitive man could have been either 'unfallen man or early fallen man,'" not an ape on its way to evolving into a man.[8]

What Lewis wrote elsewhere also argues for the view that he meant, not an ape-man human evolutionary ancestor, but rather a culturally primitive, but fully human, man. An example of his use of terms such as Neanderthal to refer to a cultural primitive people is when he delivered his inaugural lecture as professor of Medieval and Renaissance literature at Cambridge University. He also noted that "he was aware that some of his hearers didn't want 'to be lectured on Neanderthal man by a Neanderthaler, still less on dinosaurs by a dinosaur.'"[9] Lewis stated in his chapter on "The Fall of Man" in *The Problem of Pain*, that the fall "was transmitted by heredity to all generations, for it was the emergence of a new kind of man—a new species, never made by God, had sinned itself into existence."[10]

7. Lewis, *World's Last Night*, 103.

8. Lewis, *Collected Letters*, 2:207.

9. Deasy, "God, Space, and C. S. Lewis," 423.

10. Lewis, 1947, p. 71.

14

Lewis's Clear Statements Against Darwinism

Lewis also effectively argued against the Darwinistic brute, primitive ape-men idea taught by evolution. After concluding that we live in what Lewis called an absurd age, to illustrate this conclusion, he gave the example of a teacher who he thought had been teaching evolution by explaining that "in the beginning was the Ape, from whom all other life developed—including such dainties as the Brontosaurus and the Iguanodon" when "*simple people like ourselves had an idea that Darwin said* that life developed from simple organisms up to the higher plants and animals, finally to the monkey group, and from the monkey group to man." Lewis concluded that to accept both views, "you need much more *faith* in science than in theology" to believe this view called evolution.[1]

Once fully convinced that the Darwinian evolution issue was very important, Lewis was motivated to pen some of his best writings attacking the idea with gusto. Even his fictional works reflected creationism. For example, in *The Chronicles of Narnia*, Lewis's character Aslan, who represents Christ, stated the fixed categories of life existed only in the "animal Eden; there is no evolution and certainly no blurring. It is all like Genesis."[2]

An example of Lewis using the term evolution to illuminate some point which actually speaks against Darwinism is illustrated in the following quote:

1. Lewis, *Letters of C. S. Lewis*, rev. ed., 227.
2. Bloom, *C. S. Lewis*, 23.

> I should expect the next stage in Evolution not to be a stage in Evolution at all: I should expect the Evolution itself as a method of producing change will be superseded. And finally, I should not be surprised if, when the thing happened, very few people noticed that it was happening. Now, if you care to talk in these terms, the Christian view is precisely that the Next Step has already appeared. And it is really new. It is not a change from brainy men to brainier men: it is a change that goes off in a totally different direction—a change from being creatures of God to being sons of God.[3]

C. S. Lewis used the term "fall upward" in opposition to the Christian teaching of the fall of Adam. He invested much time to critique it because this idea was becoming an influential distortion of Christianity in his own day. Lewis rejected the Darwinian "fall upward" theory that Darwin argued for in his *Descent of Man*,[4] namely that humans began as immoral selfish creatures and that morality later evolved as we became social creatures. West notes that, for Lewis, Darwinism was a "purely biological theorem" that makes no cosmic, metaphysical, nor eschatological statements. West added,

> Nor can Darwinism as a scientific theory explain many of the most important aspects of biology itself: "It does not in itself explain the origin of organic life, nor of the variations, nor does it discuss the origin and validity of reason." So what *can* the Darwinian mechanism explain according to Lewis?[5]

The answer is not much. Lewis explained in his *Funeral of the Great Myth*, given that "we now have minds we can trust," evolution attempts to explain how "organic life came to exist," and "how a species that once had wings came to lose them [evolution] . . .

3. Lewis, *Mere Christianity*, 186.
4. Darwin, *Descent of Man*.
5. West, *Magician's Twin*, 124.

explains this by the negative effect of environment operating on small variations."[6] Thus, Lewis believed that

> Darwin's theory explains how a species can change over time by losing functional features it already has. Suffice to say, this is not the key thing the modern biological theory of evolution purports to explain. Noticeably absent from Lewis's description is any confidence that Darwin's unguided mechanism can account for the formation of fundamentally new forms and features in biology. Natural selection can knock out a wing, but can it build a wing in the first place? Lewis didn't seem to think so.[7]

Consequently, natural selection can explain the loss of structures, but not the gain of new structures. In a letter dated August 1, 1949, to a Miss Breckenridge, Lewis wrote, "The doctrine of Evolution is that organisms have changed, sometimes for what we call (biologically) the better . . . *quite often for what we call (biologically) the worse*."[8] In this statement he was quite correct. We now know that around 99.9 percent of all mutations are near neutral (slightly deleterious) or specifically deleterious, thus evolution is true, but going the wrong way. This background helps us to understand that Lewis's view of Darwinism is very different than that of Darwinists today. It also helps us to understand Lewis's statement that with "Darwinianism as a theorem in Biology I do not think a Christian need have any quarrel."[9]

Lewis's Growing Problem with Evolution

Lewis's other writings also document his growing problems with evolution. On September 13, 1951, he wrote to creationist Acworth, who helped him understand the implications of evolution, that "I must confess it [the information Acworth wrote on

6. Lewis, *Christian Reflections*, 86.
7. West, *Magician's Twin*, 124.
8. Lewis, *Collected Letters*, 2:962.
9. Lewis, *Present Concerns*, 63.

evolution] has shaken me: not in my belief in evolution, *which was of the vaguest and most intermittent kind*, but in my belief that the question was wholly unimportant."[10] West added that

> during the 1940s and 1950s, Lewis became more vocal about the looming dangers of what he called "scientocracy," the effort to hand over the reins of cultural and political power to an elite group of experts claiming to speak in the name of science. Lewis regarded this proposal as fundamentally subversive of a free society, and he worried about the creation of a new oligarchy that would "increasingly rely on the advice of scientists till in the end of the politicians proper become merely the scientists' puppets."[11]

This concern became increasingly dominant in Lewis's writings.

His Concerns about Natural Selection

A major problem Lewis had with evolution was with the basic foundation of orthodox Darwinism, natural selection. This idea was problematic because it violated the truth that the "incurably evolutionary or developmental character of modern thought is always urging us to forget. What is vital and healthy does not necessarily survive. Higher organisms are often conquered by lower ones. Ants as well as men are subject to accident and violent death."[12]

Lewis later added that "Darwinism gives no support to the belief that natural selection, working upon chance variations, has a general tendency to produce improvements."[13] He called the claim that Darwinian natural selection was the cause of evolution an illusion that results from observing only a few species that have been improved for human use by artificial breeding. Scientists then unscientifically extend this limited observation to the whole

10. Lewis, *Collected Letters*, 3:138; Ferngren and Numbers, "C. S. Lewis on Creation and Evolution," 72.

11. West, *Magician's Twin*, 12.

12. Lewis, *English Literature in the Sixteenth Century*, 113.

13. Lewis, *World's Last Night*, 103.

of creation.[14] Lewis concluded that, contrary to Darwinism, "there is no general law of progress in biological history."[15]

In the book *The Four Loves*, Lewis wrote that he disagreed with "those—and they are now the majority—who see human life merely as a development . . . of animal life."[16] He added that evolution teaches an idea he rejected as the following quote documents "all forms of behavior which cannot produce certificates [i.e., evidence] of an animal origin and [evidence] of survival value are suspect."[17] West stressed that "Lewis took pains to emphasize that he was not 'anti-science'" but rather was

> unequivocally opposed to *scientism*, the wrong-headed belief that modern science supplies the only reliable method of knowledge about the world, and its corollary that scientists have the right to dictate a society's morals, religious beliefs, and even government policies merely because of their scientific expertise.[18]

14. Ibid.
15. Ibid.
16. Ibid., 90.
17. Ibid.
18. West, *Magician's Twin*, 12.

15

Lewis Becomes a Militant Anti-Darwinist

As documented below, Lewis wrote much about the "myth" of what we today refer to as Darwinism in his later writings, showing that his thinking developed well beyond his early speculation and possible equivocation about evolution. One example is when Lewis traced the history of science, he noted in his usual literary style that "Darwin and Freud let the lion out of the cage," resulting in much harm to society. To illustrate this concern, Lewis wrote that the

> sciences long remained like a lion-cub whose gambols delighted its master in private; it had not yet tasted man's blood. All through the eighteenth century the tone of the common mind remained ethical, rhetorical, juristic, rather than scientific, so that [British Essayist Dr. Samuel] Johnson could truly say, "the knowledge of external nature, and the sciences which that knowledge requires or includes, are not the great or the frequent business of the human mind."[1]

It is easy to see why Lewis concluded this, namely

> Science was not the business of Man because Man had not yet become the business of science. It dealt chiefly with the inanimate . . . [until and] when Darwin starts

1. Lewis, *They Asked for a Paper*, 16–17.

> monkeying with the ancestry of Man and Freud with his soul . . . then indeed the lion will have got out of its cage.[2]

His concern was not the simple truism that the more fit were more likely to survive adverse circumstances, but "universal evolutionism," or what we refer to as the "common ancestry of all life from non-life."

Specifically, in Lewis's words, he was concerned about the "Great Myth" of evolution, namely the belief that "morality springs from savage taboos, adult sentiment from infantile sexual maladjustments, thought from instinct, mind from matter, organic from inorganic, cosmos from chaos."[3] This is not only false belief, but is also a belief that has proven to be very harmful to society. He added that this evolution of chaos to morality theory seems "immensely unplausable, because it makes the general course of nature so very unlike those parts of nature we can observe."[4] Furthermore, Lewis argued that the "Great Myth" has influenced our common thinking. He asked on what grounds

> does "latest" in advertisements mean "best"? . . . that these semantic developments owe something to the nineteenth-century belief in spontaneous progress which itself owes something either to Darwin's theorem of biological evolution or to that myth of universal evolutionism.[5]

Lewis concluded by noting that the "obviousness or naturalness which most people seem to find in the idea of emergent evolution thus seems to be a pure hallucination."[6] One of Lewis's main arguments against macroevolution as a whole, as summarized by Hooper, was as follows:

> We infer Evolution from fossils: we infer the existence of our own brains from what we find inside the skulls

2. Ibid.
3. Lewis, *Weight of Glory*, 137.
4. Ibid.
5. Lewis, *They Asked for a Paper*, 21.
6. Ibid., 164.

> of other creatures like ourselves in the dissecting room. All possible knowledge, then, depends on the validity of reasoning. If the feeling of certainty which we express by words like *must be* and *therefore* and *since* is a real perception of how things outside our own minds really "must" be, well and good. But if this certainty is merely a feeling *in* our own minds and not a genuine insight into realities beyond them—if it merely represents the way our minds happen to work—then we can have no knowledge.[7]

For these and other reasons, Lewis concluded that "a strict materialism refutes itself for the reason given long ago by Professor Haldane: 'If my mental processes are determined wholly by the motions of atoms in my brain, I have no reason to suppose that my beliefs are true, . . . hence I have no reason for supposing my brain to be composed of atoms.'"[8] Lewis concluded that science cannot determine truth by reason unless human reasoning is valid, and it

> follows that no account of the universe can be true unless that account leaves it possible for our thinking to be a real insight. A theory which explained everything else in the whole universe but which made it impossible to believe that our thinking was valid, would be utterly out of court. For our theory would itself have been reached by thinking, and if thinking is not valid that theory would, of course, be itself demolished. It would have destroyed its own credentials. It would be an argument which proved that no argument was sound—a proof that there are no such things as proofs—which is nonsense.[9]

Lewis also opposed the ultimate basic foundation of Darwinism, chance, writing that if

> the solar system was brought about by an accidental collision, then the appearance of organic life on this planet was also an accident, and the whole evolution of Man was an

7. Hooper, *C. S. Lewis*, 601.
8. Ibid., 601–2.
9. Ibid., 601.

> accident too. If so, then all our present thoughts are mere accidents—the accidental by-product of the movement of atoms. And this holds for the thoughts of the materialists and astronomers as well as for anyone else's.[10]

He added that

> if their thoughts—i.e., of materialism and astronomy—are merely accidental by-products, why should we believe them to be true? I see no reason for believing that one accident should be able to give me a correct account of all the other accidents. It's like expecting that the accidental shape taken by the splash when you upset a milk jug should give you a correct account of how the jug was made and why it was upset.[11]

The problem of personifying evolution, he wrote, is that evolution is an abstract theory

> of all biological chances (as *sphericity* is of all spherical objects) . . . not an entity in addition to particular organisms. . . . My point was that Butler, Bergson, Shaw, D. H. Lawrence etc. keep on talking as if it [evolution] *were* a thing. . . . They call it *Life*. But *life* [highest common factor] . . . can't be alive any more than *speed* can move more quickly.[12]

Lewis also recognized that, in both the scientific and general literature, evolution is often spoken of as having human traits, including intelligence, wisdom, and foresight. In a letter Lewis wrote on May 4, 1961, he accused his former doctoral student, Dr. Alastair Fowler, of "biolatry," by which he meant personalizing evolution by making it into an intelligent force, adding, "You talk of evolution as it were a substance (like individual organisms) and even a rational substance or person. I had thought it was an abstract noun."[13] Lewis added that

10. Lewis, *God in the Dock*, 41.

11. Ibid., 41–42

12. Lewis, *Collected Letters*, 3:1269.

13. Quoted in Poe and Poe, *C. S. Lewis Remembered*, 105.

> it is not impossible that, in addition to God and the individual organisms, there might be a sort of daemon, a created spirit, in the evolutionary process. But that view must surely be argued on its own merits? I mean we mustn't unconsciously and without evidence, slip into the habit of hypostatizing a noun.[14]

In his novels, Lewis created characters and situations that embody both the concepts that he feared and also those he approved. A main character in three of his novels, Elwin Ransom, was a Christian who embraces the values of pity, kindness, honesty, and respect for all individuals. In contrast, the scientist Professor Weston, in the novels *Out of the Silent Planet* and *Perelandra*, believes that there exists no absolute truth, value, or God. In both of these novels, "Weston is willing to sacrifice anyone or anything to [achieve] his goal of perpetuating human life in the universe."[15] In the novel *That Hideous Strength* the leaders of the scientific organization called the

> National Institute for Coordinated Experiments exhibit the ruthless disregard for people that Lewis feared would begin to appear in those who rejected traditional values; they would regard men as animals for experimentation, as some Nazis had so regarded the Jews. That his fears were not farfetched is seen by a brief glance at some developments in science since Lewis wrote these books.[16]

Darwinism versus Variation within the Genesis Kinds

The revolution in biology "from a devolutionary to an evolutionary scheme," Lewis explained, was "not brought about by the discovery of new facts," but rather by the "demand for a developing world—a demand obviously in harmony both with the revolutionary and

14. Hooper, *C. S. Lewis*, 496.
15. Crowell, "Theme of the Harmful Effects of Science," iv.
16. Ibid.

the romantic temper . . . when it is full grown the scientists go to work and discover the evidence."[17]

From several of Lewis's writings, both his nonfiction and fiction, Richard Cunnigham has generalized that Lewis's concern was "naturalistic empirical science must not be allowed to abrogate the right from limited empirical facts to project a whole philosophy about the nature of man and reality."[18] According to Cunningham, Lewis saw logical positivism as "the jumping-off place for naturalistic rationalism. The misuse of reason and the truncation of thought can be carried no further."[19]

In his "Funeral of a Great Myth," Lewis made one comment about Darwinian evolution, namely, he concluded, that "every age gets, within certain limits, the science it deserves," and our generation got the science it deserves, namely Darwinism and the baggage it brought with it, such as naturalism.[20] Lewis stressed that he did not "mean that these new phenomena [such as those observed in biology] are illusionary," but believed that nature contains all sorts of phenomena that can be cherry picked to "suit many different tastes" and theories.[21]

Lewis stressed that the doctrine of evolution "is certainly a hypothesis," although currently the best hypothesis produced by biologists, but a hypothesis nonetheless and not a fact, adding it may be shown "by later biologists, to be a less satisfactory hypothesis than was hoped fifty years ago."[22] Lewis then noted that microevolution, or variation within the Genesis kinds, should be distinguished "from what may be called the universal evolutionism" by which he means

> the belief that the very formula of universal process is from imperfect to perfect, from small beginnings to great endings, from the rudimentary to the elaborate: the

17. Lewis, *Discarded Image*, 220–21.
18. Cunningham, *Defender of the Faith*, 52.
19. Ibid., 53.
20. Lewis, *Christian Reflections*, 85.
21. Ibid.
22. Ibid., 83, 85.

> belief which makes people find it natural to think that morality springs from savage taboos, adult sentiment from infantile sexual maladjustments, thought from instinct, mind from matter, organic from inorganic, cosmos from chaos. This is perhaps the deepest habit of mind in the contemporary world.[23]

Lewis also argued for an eternal God by reasoning that "there was never a time when nothing existed; otherwise nothing would exist now."[24] Furthermore, "creation," as applied to humans, is "an entirely misleading term" for the reason that we as humans can only *rearrange* what God has created because no *vestige* of real creativity *de novo* exists in us: "Try to imagine a new primary colour, a third sex, a fourth dimension, or even a monster which does not consist of bits of existing animals stuck together . . . we are [merely] recombining elements made by Him and already containing *His* meanings."[25]

In a biography of Lewis, Clyde Kilby, after noting "the accusation that Lewis despises science" clarifies this change by noting that "what he actually dislikes is 'scientism' or the popular unthinking assumption that there is no truth other than truth revealed by the scientific method." To support this he quoted in Lewis's essay "On Obstinacy in Belief,"[26] that

> distinguishes between scientific and Christian thought. Scientists, he says, are less concerned with "believing" things than simply finding this out. When you find something out, you do not any longer say you believe it, any more than you would say you believe the multiplication table.[27]

The fact is, materialistic scientists endeavor to escape from unbelief by turning

23. Lewis, *Weight of Glory*, 104.

24. Lewis, *Miracles*, 141

25. Lewis, letter dated February 20, 1943, in *Collected Letters*, 2:555. Also Lewis, *Letters of C. S. Lewis*, 203.

26. Kilby, *Christian World of C. S. Lewis*; from Lewis, *World's Last Night*.

27. Kilby, *Christian World of C. S. Lewis*, 175–76.

> belief into knowledge. Lewis defines belief as "assent to a proposition which we think so overwhelmingly probable that there is a psychological exclusion of doubt, though not a logical exclusion of dispute." The scientist himself holds "beliefs" of this sort concerning his wife . . . which though not wholly subject to laboratory demonstration assume a large measure of evidence.[28]

He adds that it is wrong "to think that the obstinacy of Christians in their belief is like that of a poor scientist doggedly attempting to preserve a hypothesis although the evidence is against him"[29] and that their

> obstinacy is more like that of the confidence of a child who is told by its mother that to ease the pain from a thorn in its finger it must undergo the additional pain of removal. That confidence rests not in a scientific demonstration concerning the mother but in confidence, even emotional confidence, in her as a person.[30]

The reality is, if an injured child acts on his or her "'unbelief' and refuses to let its mother touch the finger, then no 'mighty work' can be done. Yet if it acts on its confidence the thorn will be got rid of and an increasing confidence in the mother will be established."[31] Likewise, "Christian doctrine requires us to put confidence in God who, being infinitely superior to us, will sometimes appear unreasonable to us, but in whom, as with the child and its mother, confidence yields the results promised."[32] He adds that in Lewis's reply to Professor Haldane, Lewis argues,

> The sciences are "good and innocent in themselves," though evil "scientism" is creeping into them. And finally what we are obviously up against throughout the story is not scientists but officials. If anyone ought to feel himself libeled by this book it is not the scientist but

28. Ibid.
29. Ibid.
30. Ibid.
31. Ibid.
32. Ibid.

> the civil servant: and, next to the civil servant, certain philosophers.[33]

This is exactly what is occurring today.

Lewis's Increasing Strident Opposition to Evolutionary Naturalism

Lewis was most critical of the central thesis of Darwinism, its core foundational belief, namely naturalism. Darwinists attempt to show, through both science and reasoning based on naturalism, that our world and its inhabitants can be fully explained as the product of a mindless and purposeless system that evolved due to chance, time, and the operation of the laws of physics and chemistry. Lewis strongly opposed this whole idea using both science and reason. He taught that the something which exists beyond the material world is what we call the supernatural and that humans are on the borderline between

> the Natural and Supernatural. Material events cannot produce spiritual activity, but the latter can be responsible for many of our actions on Nature. Will and Reason cannot depend on anything but themselves, but Nature can depend on Will and Reason, or, in other words, God created Nature.[34]

Furthermore, Lewis taught that what today is called intelligent design is manifest in the relation between nature and supernature which becomes intelligible only

> if the Supernatural made the Natural. We even have an idea of this making, since we know the power of imagination, though we can create nothing new, but can only rearrange our material provided through sense data. It is not inconceivable that the universe was created by an

33. Lewis, *On Stories*, 71.
34. Lewis, *God in the Dock*, 276.

> Imagination [God] strong enough to impose phenomena on other minds.[35]

Although it appears that Lewis may have equivocated on evolution as early as 1925, his strong personal views against naturalism were clear from the date of his conversion to his death in 1963. In a letter to his father dated August 1925, Lewis wrote: "It will be a comfort to me all my life to know that the scientist and the materialist have not the last word: that Darwin and [evolutionist Herbert] Spencer undermining ancestral beliefs stand themselves on a foundation of sand . . . [and have created] gigantic assumptions and irreconcilable contradictions an inch below the surface" of the theory.[36]

Along this line he also wrote, "One cause of misery and vice is always present with us in the greed and pride of men, but at certain periods in history this [problem] is greatly increased by the temporary prevalence of some false philosophy."[37]

This "false philosophy" was Darwinism that Lewis has effectively questioned by asking how a brain that evolved can be trusted to determine if that which made it, evolution, were true. Lewis stressed that we must "infer Evolution from fossils" and that "all possible knowledge . . . depends on the validity of reasoning," and thus, unless "human reasoning is valid no science can be true."[38] He observed that, after studying the biological world, scientists had begun to study humans in the same way. Before this scientists had assumed their own worldview, and through it had

> seen all other things. Now, his own reason has become the object: it is as if we took out our eyes to look at them. Thus studied, his own reason appears to him as the epiphenomenon which accompanies chemical or electrical events in a cortex which is itself the by-product of a blind evolutionary process. His own logic, hitherto the king whom events in all possible worlds must obey, become

35. Ibid.
36. Lewis, *Collected Letters*, 1:213.
37. Lewis, *Christian Reflections*, 72.
38. Lewis, *Miracles*, 21.

> merely subjective. There is no reason for supposing that it yields truth.[39]

Furthermore, because God created the natural world by creating

> it out of His love and artistry—it demands our reverence; because it is only a creature and not He, it is, from another point of view, of little account. And still more, because Nature, and especially human nature, is fallen, it must be corrected and the evil within it must be mortified. But its essence is good.[40]

Reppert presented the logically sequential development of Lewis's thought in which he [Reppert] demonstrated—contrary to the dismissals of critics—that the basic thrust of Lewis's argument against Darwinism can stand up to modern philosophical scrutiny.[41] For example, one of Lewis's more important works, *Miracles*, contains one of his most powerful critiques of the worldview that is at the foundation of both Darwinism and humanism, namely naturalism.

Specifically, in his *Miracles* book, Lewis wrote that believers in naturalism assume that life "was not designed" because they do not believe that an Intelligent Designer exists. He then documented the fact that naturalism and naturalistic evolution are, at their core, atheism.[42] A concern Lewis often broached in his writing was the relationship between science and the government, possibly because Hitler and his government often abused science, specifically social Darwinism and eugenics. An example is Lewis wrote in response:

> "Under modern conditions any effective invitation to Hell will certainly appear in the guise of scientific planning"—as Hitler's regime in fact did. Every tyrant must begin by claiming to have what his victims respect and to give what they want. The majority [of people] in most modern countries respect science and want [government]

39. Lewis, *Christian Reflections*, 72.
40. Lewis, *God in the Dock*, 148.
41. Reppert, *C. S. Lewis's Dangerous Idea.*
42. Lewis, *Miracles*, 27–28.

> to be planned. And, therefore, almost by definition, if any man or group wishes to enslave us it will of course describe itself as "scientific planned democracy."[43]

Hitler believed that producing a "pure race" was necessary to insure the future of the Aryan race. An example Lewis provided to support his [Lewis's] view is the emergence of some political parties "in the modern sense—the Fascists, Nazis, or Communists." What distinguishes this modern political form "from the political parties of the nineteenth century is the belief of its members that they are not merely trying to carry out a programme, but are obeying an impersonal force: that Nature, or Evolution, or the Dialectic, or the Race, is carrying them on."[44] Lewis admits that sometimes the actual state of affairs of the people can "be so bad that a man is tempted to risk change even by revolutionary methods" because

> desperate diseases require desperate remedies and that necessity knows no law. But to yield to this temptation is, I think, fatal. It is under that pretext that every abomination enters. Hitler, the Machiavellian Prince, the Inquisition, the Witch Doctor, all claimed to be necessary.[45]

43. Lewis, *On Stories*, 74–75.
44. Ibid., 78.
45. Ibid., 77.

16

The Funeral of the Great Myth

IN AN ESSAY TITLED "The Funeral of a Great Myth," Lewis explained why he regarded Darwinian evolution as the "great Myth of nineteenth and early twentieth Century," a myth that he wanted to bury.[1] He even called "the Evolutionary Myth" a tragedy due to its fruit, such as eugenics.[2] Lewis wrote that the "central idea of the myth is what its believers would call 'Evolution' or 'Development' or 'Emergence'" of higher life from lower life forms.[3] In 1951, Lewis wrote that he was now inclined to think that evolution was "*the* central and radical lie in the whole web of falsehood that now governs" modern civilization.[4]

Evolutionary naturalism, Lewis explained, is "not the logical result of what is vaguely called 'modern science,'" but rather is a picture of reality that has resulted, not from empirical evidence, but from imagination.[5] Furthermore, Lewis notes in *Mere Christianity* that most people believe in many things including "evolution" on the basis of authority "because the scientists say so" and not on the basis of fact and scientific knowledge.[6] Lewis concluded that evolution theory emerged long before the necessary scientific

1. Lewis, *Christian Reflections*, 82.
2. Ibid., 84.
3. Ibid., 83.
4. Lewis, *Collected Letters*, 3:138; Ferngren and Numbers, "C. S. Lewis on Creation," 29–30.
5. Lewis, *Christian Reflections*, 82.
6. Lewis, *Mere Christianity*, 63.

research had been completed and, in making the myth, imagination has, and still does today, run ahead of the scientific evidence.[7]

Furthermore, Lewis argued, evolution infects minds as different as professors and media personalities such as Walt Disney and "is implicit in nearly every modern article on politics, sociology, and ethics."[8] It has even infected English literature, such as that by H. G. Wells and Robert Browning.[9] Lewis stressed that the myth is bolstered by selecting facts from scientific theories, cherry-picking facts that are "modified . . . in obedience to [the] imaginative and emotional needs" of the Darwinists.[10]

Lewis was especially concerned with the harm done by the "disingenuousness of orthodox biologists" in pushing evolutionary naturalism.[11] Although Lewis admired much of the English literature that is based on the evolution myth, he had a major problem with its implications and its advocates forcing it on the public, writing that the evolution myth "has great allies, / Its friends are propaganda, party cries, / And bilge, and Man's incorrigible mind."[12]

His concern about natural selection is also shown through in his novels, which include both good and bad spirits. Weston, a character in one of Lewis's novels, who is a nonbeliever scientist, "sees God and His angels as symbolic of the goal toward which evolution is striving and the Devil and his angels as the driving force behind the upward struggle [writing]; 'Your Devil and your God are both pictures of the same force.'"[13]

Lewis's criticism was not of science in general, "but of science without values, of science which makes itself God."[14] One of England's great modern scientists, J. B. S. Haldane, "charged that

7. Lewis, *Christian Reflections*, 84.

8. Ibid., 82.

9. Irvine, "The Influence of Darwin."

10. Lewis, *Christian Reflections*, 83.

11. Ferngren and Numbers, "C. S. Lewis on Creation," 30.

12. Lewis, *Christian Reflections*, 112.

13. Lewis, *Perelandra*, 93.

14. Crowell, "Theme of the Harmful Effects of Science," 27.

Lewis traduced scientists in *That Hideous Strength*."[15] Lewis replied to Haldane by charging that, if any of his novels "could be plausibly accused of being a libel on scientists it would be *Out of the Silent Planet*,"[16] which he admits is certainly an attack, but

> not on scientists, yet on something which might be called "scientism"—a certain outlook on the world which is usually connected with the popularization of the sciences, though it is much less common among real scientists than among their readers. It is, in a word, the belief that the supreme moral end is the perpetuation of our own species, and that this is to be pursued even if, in the process of being fitted for survival, our species has to be stripped of all those things for which we value it—of pity, of happiness, and of freedom.[17]

One of Lewis's characters zealously opposed Bergson's creative evolution theory, which illustrates what

> Lewis had in mind when he wrote to Haldane of the danger of placing political power and scientific planning in the hands of those who felt that they had a mission to carry out. . . . The horrors of the Inquisition, the Salem witch trials, the crushing of Hus's life and work in Bohemia and of Wycliffe's in England, as well as communism's ruthless destruction of opponents in this century—all these are examples of this union of power and passionate belief which Lewis feared, but they lacked the power now known to science.[18]

One example where science has abused its power in the West is the movement to crush all efforts, both by intelligent design supporters, and all forms of theistic creationists, to do research and assume a place at the table of ideas. They are now largely ghettoized and cut off from mainline science.[19]

15. Ibid.
16. Hooper, *C. S. Lewis*, 76.
17. Ibid., 76–77.
18. Crowell, "Theme of the Harmful Effects of Science," 67.
19. Bergman, *Slaughter of the Dissidents*.

Lewis Not Antiscience

As documented above, the claim is common that because Lewis opposed scientism and Darwinism, therefore he was antiscience. After noting the very real attractions of Lewis's trilogy, one must consider an aspect of it that "for many readers prove an insuperable stumbling block. That is his total and unrelenting attack on science. It doesn't suffice to protest that that attack is against godless scientism."[20] In his trilogy books

> there is no other science but the godless and dehumanizing, nor any other kind of scientist than those of the N.I.C.E.'s Power Elite, "dragging up from its shallow and unquiet grave the old dream of Man as God," men who, as is said of one of them, "had passed from Hegel into Hume, thence through Pragmatism, and then through Logical Positivism and out at last into the complete void."[21]

Although Lewis was anti-evolutionism or, in his terminology, an antidevelopmentalist, he was not antiscience, but believed that "all scientific theories are tentative and as dependent on changing presuppositions and climates of opinion as on new empirical data."[22]

Lewis wrote that evolution in true science is only a hypothesis about the changes that we observe every day in nature called microevolution, a view with which he had no problems. Conversely, in the popular mind the myth is believed to be a "*fact about improvements*" in living organisms, a view that he strongly objected to.[23] The popular view of evolution involves common ancestry, life moving "upward and onward," an idea that Lewis also rejected. He added that "if science offers any instances that seems to satisfy" the belief that life is evolving upward, that idea "will be eagerly

20. Deasy, "God, Space, and C. S. Lewis," 422.

21. Ibid.

22. Quoted in Ferngren and Numbers, "C. S. Lewis on Creation," 31.

23. Lewis, *Christian Reflections*, 85.

accepted. If it offers any instances that frustrate it [this view], they will simply be ignored."[24]

Lewis repeatedly stressed that the findings of science were not the final truth, but that science progresses and develops, requiring one to be knowledgeable about some specific science topic.[25] One must keep up-to-date because what is accepted today may be outdated tomorrow. Likewise, Christian apologists must answer the current, very negative attitude of the behavioral sciences against Christianity. This attitude is based on Lewis's fear that "the science which rejects or destroys traditional morality," which is primarily found

> in those disciplines which he once called "pseudo-sciences," for example, sociology, and behaviorist and Freudian psychology (especially where scholars in these areas of study try to enter philosophy and religion without the necessary training and study). He makes a clear distinction between these groups and the pure sciences like chemistry and mathematics in the novel already mentioned.[26]

Lewis also noted that Christians must be cautious about using science to defend Christianity because that which scientists adopted may be proven wrong one hundred years from now because:

> Science is in continual change and we must try to keep abreast of it. For the same reason, we must be very cautious of snatching at any scientific theory which, for the moment, seems to be in our favour. We may *mention* such thing; but we must mention them . . . without claiming that they are more than "interesting."[27]

He added that sentences beginning with the expression "science has now proved"

> should be avoided. If we try to base our apologetic on some recent development in science, we shall usually

24. Ibid., 86.
25. Dickerson and O'Hara, *Narnia and the Fields of Arbol.*
26. Crowell, "Theme of the Harmful Effects of Science, 26–27.
27. Lewis, *God in the Dock*, 92.

> find that just as we have put the finishing touches to our argument science has changed its mind and quietly withdrawn the theory we have been using as our foundation stone. *Timeo Danaos et dona ferentes* [I fear the Greeks even when they bear gifts] is a sound principle.[28]

Lewis concluded that evolutionary naturalism is "immensely implausible because it makes the general course of nature so very unlike those parts of nature we can observe."[29] Referring to the "chicken or the egg" question, Lewis wrote that moderns acquiescence to "universal evolutionism is a kind of optical illusion, produced by attending exclusively" to the "does the chicken come from the egg or the egg from the chicken" problem, adding, in support of intelligent design, that we "are taught from childhood to notice" how the oak tree

> grows from the acorn and to forget that the acorn itself was dropped by a perfect oak. We are reminded constantly that the adult human being was an embryo, never that the life of the embryo came from two adult human beings. We love to notice that the express engine of today is the descendant of the "Rocket"; we do not equally remember that the "Rocket" springs not from some even more rudimentary engine, but from something much more perfect and complicated than itself—namely, a man of genius. The obviousness or naturalness which most people seem to find in the idea of emergent evolution thus seems to be a pure hallucination.[30]

His point is that both of these examples are not evidence for evolutionary naturalism, but rather are they the result of innovation and creation due to intelligent design.[31] The growth of a tree from a seed was programmed by design, and, likewise, the invention and improvement of mechanical machinery was a result of design due to human intelligence. Neither evolved by random

28. Ibid.
29. Lewis, *Weight of Glory*, 104.
30. Ibid., 104–5.
31. Lewis, *Christian Reflections*, 90.

chance and mutations, the mechanism of orthodox evolutionism, but rather both came about by the opposite means, namely intelligent design. Lewis added that

> since the egg-bird-egg sequence leads us to no plausible beginning, is it not reasonable to look for the real origin somewhere outside [of the] sequence altogether? You have to go outside the sequence of engines, into the world of men, to find the real originator of the Rocket. Is it not equally reasonable to look outside Nature for the real Originator of the natural order?[32]

This "Originator of the natural order" is the Intelligent Creator called, in English, God. Under the subtitle "all the guess work which masquerades as 'Science,'" Lewis wrote that a scientific hypothesis "establishes itself by a cumulative process: or, to use popular language, if you make the same guess often enough it ceases to be a guess and becomes a Scientific Fact."[33] He added that our world is being bombarded with the evolutionism myth in hundreds of ways, including in schools, books, museums, newscasts, and the media as a whole.

Thus, Darwinism has become established in the West, not by evidence, but because it has been repeated *ad infinitum* in both the scientific and popular literature. Although Lewis once admitted that his knowledge of paleontology and geology was limited, he was able to make judgments on Darwinism based on viewing the whole Darwinian philosophy as a worldview, which it is.[34] One of Lewis's most telling illustrations of the illogical aspect of evolution was presented under the heading "Evolution and Comparative Religion," where he discusses the basic problems of the "palaeontological evidence" for evolution.[35]

32. Lewis, *God in the Dock*, 211.
33. Lewis, *Pilgrim's Regress*, 22.
34. Lewis, *Collected Letters*, 2:848.
35. Lewis, *Pilgrim's Regress*, 21.

Twisting the Facts

Lewis specifically objected to twisting facts so that they fit into the evolution myth, such as changing microevolution from "a theory of change into a theory of improvement," thus turning evolution into a theory that explains all of creation, namely macroevolution, the theory that not

> merely terrestrial organisms but *everything* is moving "upwards and onwards." Reason has "evolved" out of instinct, virtue out of complexes, poetry out of erotic howls and grunts, civilization out of savagery, the organic out of inorganic, the solar system out of some sidereal soup.[36]

Lewis concluded that this theory of evolution is not a deduction from the *data* using the accepted scientific method, but rather is a product of *imagination*. The human mind is all too easily convinced of its validity because many people *prefer* to believe that we, and our generation, are better than our parents and our parents better than theirs, and that any theory which seems to reinforce this belief, such as evolution, appeals to us.[37] In fact, humans tend to believe what we *want* to believe, and the evidence is often secondary, if that.

Lewis also twice quoted Professor Watson, once with reservations, who wrote that evolution "is accepted by zoologists not because it has been observed to occur or . . . can be proved by logically coherent evidence to be true, but because the only alternative, special creation, is clearly incredible."[38] In another essay, after again quoting Watson, Lewis asked rhetorically, "Does the whole vast structure of modern naturalism depend not on positive evidence but simply on an *a priori* metaphysical prejudice? Was it devised not to get the facts but to keep out God?"[39] He answered this question in his writings, concluding that this clearly was the case.

36. Lewis, *Christian Reflections*, 86.

37. Ibid., 82.

38. Ibid., 85.

39. Lewis, *Weight of Glory*, 104.

Lewis went so far as to state indications exist that "biologists are already contemplating a withdrawal from the whole Darwinian position."[40] One reason he gave for this conclusion was the fact that "what Darwin really accounted for was not the origin, but the elimination of species"[41] by natural selection.

40. Lewis, *World's Last Night*, 101.

41. Ibid.

17

Science Supports a Creation Worldview

Lewis saw that the overthrow of the once widespread belief that the universe had always existed supported the Christian view that the universe was created by God. He writes that modern physics has proven the "universe had a beginning." In contrast,

> the great materialistic systems of the past all believed in the eternity, and thence in the self-existence of matter. As Professor Whittaker said in the Ridell Lectures of 1942, "It was never possible to oppose seriously the dogma of the Creation except by maintaining that the world has existed from all eternity in more or less its present state." This fundamental ground for materialism has now been withdrawn. We should not lean too heavily on this, for scientific theories change. But at the moment it appears that the burden of proof rests, not on us, but on those who deny that nature has some cause beyond herself.[1]

This cause beyond nature, Lewis concluded, is the Intelligent Designer we call God.

Lewis was also very

> aware that Darwinism has often functioned as a religion in itself. It certainly functioned that way for Thomas Huxley, "Darwin's bulldog." Evolution was a religion for politically varied figures such as playwright George Bernard Shaw, philosopher Fredrich Nietzsche, and composer Richard Strauss. Popular understanding of

1. Lewis, *God in the Dock*, 39.

> evolution actually owes much more to them than to Darwinian biologists.[2]

Furthermore, each one of these writers had their

> own ideas about what evolution, specifically human evolution, was. However, Shaw got it right at least once. He explained in *Back to Methuselah* that "if this sort of selection could turn an antelope into a giraffe, it could conceivably turn a pond full of amoebas into the French academy." That, precisely, is what Darwin and his successors believe, and what everyone who can be described as a non-Darwinist disbelieves.[3]

Nor was Lewis very impressed with the common argument that Darwinism is beyond doubt because it is the consensus of scientists, or what Lewis calls the "climate of opinion." Whether the issue is evolution or the current strident opposition to intelligent design, Lewis argued that it is not sufficient simply to acquiesce to the current "climate of opinion." In *The Problem of Pain* he wrote that "I take a very low view of 'climates of opinion,'" noting that discoveries are both often made by, and the "errors corrected by, those who *ignore* the 'climate of opinion.'"[4]

Lewis's "fears of what man might do to mankind" includes his study of certain trends in modern thought. The first trend of importance that he listed was the modernist view "that morality is relative and that moral standards have grown from mere impulses, from chemical reactions and responses which are in turn simply part of the irrational, blind development of organic life from the inorganic."[5] The second trend he feared

> is the idea that man will and should completely conquer nature, even human nature. The combined effect of these two ideas, Lewis feared, will spell the end of mankind as we know it . . . objective morality will have no guide but

2. O'Leary, *By Design or by Chance?*, 64.
3. Ibid.
4. Lewis, *They Asked for a Paper*, 134.
5. Crowell, "Theme of the Harmful Effects," 12.

> their own feelings and desires when they begin to control human nature.[6]

Specifically, he had in mind the adverse moral results "by eugenics, by pre-natal conditioning, and by an education and propaganda based on a perfect applied psychology."[7]

The Commercial World Welcomes the Myth

Lewis reasoned that advertisers welcome the myth because it reinforced the belief that *the new model supersedes the old*, and therefore must be an improved model, more economical, or better in other ways. Likewise, a powerful reason why politicians want to keep the myth alive is because they want us to believe that their economic and fiscal packages are better than the previous ones. This was seen in both the 2008 and 2012 American election's stress on "change" advertised by both parties, especially the Democrats as "change we can believe in."

Lewis stressed that, although the myth is "nonsense . . . a man would be a dull dog if he could not feel the thrill and charm of it."[8] Nonetheless, Lewis's advice is to "treat the Myth with respect" because the myth

> gives us almost everything the imagination craves—irony, heroism, vastness, unity in multiplicity, and a tragic close. It appeals to every part of me except my reason. That is why those of us who feel that the Myth is already dead for us *must not make the mistake of trying to "debunk" it in the wrong way*. We must not fancy that we are securing the modern world from something grim and dry, something that starves the soul. The contrary is the truth. It is our painful duty to wake the world from an enchantment.[9]

6. Ibid.
7. Lewis, *Abolition of Man*, 72.
8. Lewis, *Christian Reflections*, 93.
9. Ibid., emphasis added.

Lewis concludes that he grew up believing the evolutionary naturalism myth, and he once felt—and still feels—"it's almost perfect grandeur":

> Let no one say we are in an unimaginative age: neither the Greeks nor the Norsemen ever invented a better story. Even to the present day, in certain moods, I could almost find it in my heart to wish that it was not mythical, but true. And yet, how could it be?[10]

After Lewis studied the myth in detail, he concluded that he could not accept it because he cannot accept the claim that humans, and human reason, are "simply the unforeseen and unintended by-product of a mindless process [existing] at one stage of its endless and aimless becoming." One reason is because the myth itself negates the only grounds on which the myth could possibly be true—reason.[11] He concluded, "For my own part, though, I believe it [the Myth] no longer."[12] Another example Lewis cites that negates the macroevolution myth is the wonder of the human mind, noting that

> the Myth asks me to believe that reason is simply the unforeseen and unintended by-product of a mindless process at one stage of its endless and aimless becoming. The content of the Myth thus knocks from under me the only ground on which I could possibly believe the Myth to be true. If my own mind is a product of the irrational—if what seem my clearest reasoning are only the way in which a creature conditioned as I am is bound to feel—how shall I trust my mind when it tells me about Evolution?[13]

In Reppert's book *C. S. Lewis's Dangerous Idea* noted above, Reppert documents that Lewis effectively demonstrated that the Darwinian argument was circular. If materialism or naturalism were true, then scientific reasoning itself could not be trusted. Reppert adds, if we take our obligation to share our Christian faith

10. Ibid., 88.
11. Ibid., 89.
12. Ibid., 93.
13. Ibid., 89.

seriously, Lewis showed that we will realize that the Myth is a very real impediment for Christian evangelism today, both behind the scenes and out in the open.

Lewis notes that one evil of evolutionary naturalism is it argues "that moral codes are simply subjective values [that] evolved as people have developed through an evolutionary process from mindless matter is to say that we have no basis for choosing to call any idea good or bad or even to trust our own reasoning."[14] As Lewis illustrated in his novel *That Hideous Strength*,

> many a mild-eyed scientist in pince-nez, many a popular dramatist, many an amateur philosopher in our midst, means in the long run just the same as the Nazi rulers of Germany. Traditional values are to be "debunked" and mankind to be cut into some fresh shape at the will of some few lucky people in one lucky generation which has learned how to do it.[15]

Lewis Censors His Antievolution Views

A major source of Lewis's anti-Darwinism views was in his manuscript titled "The Myth," which was not published until after he died. A second major source were his unpublished letters to Captain Acworth, president of the British Evolution Protest Movement.[16]

Lewis was far less open in public than in private about his opposition to evolution for several reasons. First, he was not a biologist and wanted to avoid openly confronting biologists because he felt somewhat insecure in the natural science field. For this reason, he attacked evolutionary naturalism in his writings largely from the perspective of philosophy.

Second, he realized that actively attacking evolution would produce much opposition to his person and writings and, as a result, would detract from his main work, Christian apologetics.

14. Crowell, "Theme of the Harmful Effects," 26.
15. Ibid., 24–25; quote from *Abolition of Man*, 85.
16. Ferngren and Numbers, "C. S. Lewis on Creation."

Third, very early in his career he may have flirted with theistic evolution, including common descent, and only after he explored the issue in some detail did he come to have major doubts about Darwinism. Finally, he did produce a well-reasoned book against naturalism, the book *Miracles*, which was his major concern.[17] This book is still in print and is considered one of his most important works. The result of this conflict was that, for his entire life,

> Lewis remained reticent about speaking publicly on evolution. His three great apologetic works from the 1940s dealt with human origins only briefly and where absolutely necessary. Lewis believed he would do little good taking on a controversial subject in which he was not an expert. It is clear, however, from letters and essays that remained unpublished during his lifetime that Lewis did much reading and thinking in private about evolution. Until the 1950s, he tried to find a middle ground, accepting the "biological theorem" while rejecting its "metaphysical statements." In the 1950s he grew more skeptical [of evolution]. Between 1944 and 1960, he corresponded privately with Bernard Acworth (1885–1963), one of Britain's leading antievolutionists.[18]

Nonetheless, Lewis did teach creationism in many of his books, even if only indirectly. For example, he wrote that "when God made space and worlds that move in space, and clothed our world with air, and gave us such eyes and such imaginations as those we have, He knew what the sky would mean to us. And since nothing in His work is accidental, if He knew, He intended."[19] Lewis was firmly convinced that "at least three things, joy, ethics, and human reason, . . . could not have evolved [and in] . . . the introductory chapter to *The Problem of Pain*, Lewis adds a fourth—religion."[20]

He also opined that "we finite beings may apprehend" God because "His glory [has been translated] into multiple forms—into

17. Lewis, *Miracles*.

18. Schultz et al., *Encyclopedia of Religion*, 158–59.

19. Lewis, *Miracles*, 258.

20. Markos, *Lewis Agonistes*, 48.

stars, woods, waters, beasts, and the bodies of men" and it is in them—evidence for the argument from design—that we see the proof for the existence of God.[21] The implications of this view are obvious, namely, if you cannot accept the view

> that the whole universe is a mere mechanical dance of atoms, it is nice to be able to think of this great mysterious Force rolling on through the centuries and carrying you on its crest. If, on the other hand, you want to do something rather shabby, the Life-Force, being only a blind force, with no morals and no mind, will never interfere with you like that troublesome God we learned about when we were children.[22]

As noted, when he learned more about nature and the world, Lewis became increasingly hostile toward orthodox evolution. One example is a poem about evolution titled "The Evolutionary Hymn" in which Lewis applied his consummate skills to mock evolution as a result of the fact that, in the 1950s, he not only "grew more skeptical" of evolution, but also more hostile to it. In 1951

> his doubts about evolution were being stimulated by the "fanatical twisted attitudes of its defenders." In 1957 he made his only public attack on the theory. In a poem titled "Evolutionary Hymn" he mocked evolution's pretensions to be a religion leading us "Up the future's endless stair."[23]

The complete poem is a follows

> Lead us, Evolution, lead us
> Up the future's endless stair:
> Chop us, change us, prod us, weed us,
> For stagnation is despair:
> Groping, guessing, yet progressing,
> Lead us nobody knows where.

21. Williams and Lewis, *Taliessin through Logres*, 291.
22. Lewis, *Mere Christianity*, 35.
23. Schultz et al., *Encyclopedia of Religion*, 158–59.

Wrong or justice in the present,
Joy or sorrow, what are they
While there's always jam to-morrow
While we tread the onward way?
Never knowing where we're going,
We can never go astray.

To whatever variation
Our posterity may turn
Hairy, squashy, or crustacean,
Bulbous-eyed or square of stern,
Tusked or toothless, mild or ruthless,
Towards that unknown god we yearn.

Ask not if it's god or devil,
Brethren, lest your words imply
Static norms of good and evil
(As in Plato) throned on high;
Such scholastic, inelastic,
Abstract yardsticks we deny.

Far too long have sages vainly
Glossed great Nature's simple text;
He who runs can read it plainly,
"Goodness = what comes next."
By evolving, Life is solving
All the questions we perplexed.

On then! Value means survival—
Value. If our progeny
Spreads and spawns and licks each rival,
That will prove its deity
(Far from pleasant, by our present
Standards, though it well may be).[24]

24. Hooper, *C. S. Lewis*, 176.

It is significant that Lewis published this poem in the 1957 *Cambridge Review* under the pseudonym "Nat Whilk."[25] It was also only after Lewis's death that his two essays written in the 1940s which contain his strong views against Darwinism and macroevolution were published, namely "A Reply to Professor Haldane" and "The Funeral of a Great Myth."

This fact also indicates that he had strong objections to macroevolution long before he died. The use of a pseudonym and delaying publications of his poem mocking Darwinism supports the view that he did not want to face the wrath of the Darwin establishment. This fact also is supported by a letter that Lewis wrote to Acworth penned in 1951. In this letter Lewis "politely declined to write a preface for one of Acworth's books, pointing out that, as a 'popular Apologist,'" he had to be careful because so many of his opposers were looking for "things that might discredit him."[26]

Those who take the position that Lewis was an evolutionist attempt to claim that this poem was not meant to be taken literally, or that Lewis was speaking about the philosophy of evolution, not literal molecules to mankind evolution. This is a common approach used in an effort to claim, for example, that the account of Adam and Eve cannot be taken literally, but is symbolic of all humanity. If the poem is symbolic, what possibly is it symbolic of? Those who support this position have never given a plausible explanation, except it could not be literal. The words in the first six lines of the poem are a poetic description of Darwinism, which teaches that simple organic molecules evolved into higher and higher forms of life, eventually leading to simple single celled animals, fish, reptiles, mammals, primates and, eventually evolved into the highest form of life, humans. It cannot reasonably be understood in any other way.

Some of Lewis's most cutting remarks about evolution were derived from his own academic background, literature, and he freely used literary phraseology to make his point. For example, an article he wrote in 1944 mocking evolution indicates that he

25. Schultz et al., *Encyclopedia of Religion*, 159.

26. Ibid., 69.

had grave doubts about Darwinism long before the late 1950s. He wrote in his book *They Asked for a Paper* that we should consider the enormous claim of Christianity's

> chief contemporary rival—what we may loosely call the Scientific Outlook, the picture of Mr. Wells [a leading expositor of evolution in Lewis's day] and the rest [of the evolutionists]. Is it not one of the finest myths which human imagination has yet produced? The play [the evolution story] is preceded by the most austere of all preludes: the infinite void, and matter restlessly moving to bring forth it knows not what. Then, by the millionth millionth chance—what tragic irony—the conditions at one point of space and time bubble up into that tiny fermentation which is the beginning of life.[27]

He then added in the novel the observation that everything appears "to be against the infant hero of our drama," but in the end life somehow wins with

> infinite suffering, against all but insuperable obstacles, it spreads, it breeds, it complicates itself: from the amoeba up to the plant, up to the reptile, up to the mammal. We glance briefly at the age of monsters. Dragons prowl the earth, devour one another and die.[28]

In the book *Miracles*, Lewis reasoned

> that the birth of modern science and its belief in the regularity of nature depended on the Judeo-Christian view of God as Creator: "Men became scientific because they expected Law in Nature, and they expected Law in Nature because they believed in a Legislator" [Lewis, *Miracles*, 106]. Nevertheless, Lewis thought that biology after Darwin provided potent fuel for turning science into a secular religion.[29]

27. Lewis, *They Asked for a Paper*, 154–55.
28. Ibid.
29. West, *Magician's Twin*, 21.

An example is, according to what Lewis called this "fairy-tale," humans evolved by the same process as did animals, thus were animals. He adds as the weak spark of the first

> life began amidst the huge hostilities of the inanimate, so now again, amidst the beasts that are far larger and stronger than he, there comes forth a little naked, shivering, cowering creature, shuffling, not yet erect, promising nothing: the product of another millionth millionth chance. . . . He becomes the Cave Man with his club and his flints, muttering and growling over his enemies' bones, dragging his screaming mate by her hair (I could never quite make out why), tearing his children to pieces in fierce jealousy till one of them is old enough to tear him, cowering before the terrible gods whom he has created in his own image. But these are only growing pains. Wait till the next Act.[30]

Lewis continues with the next Act in what he called "this tale," in which the harm of the myth becomes obvious in the form of eugenics, Freudian psychology, and communism. He wrote that Darwinism teaches that mankind is evolving into the true Man, learning to

> master nature. Science comes and dissipates the superstitions of his infancy [religion, creationism, and God]. More and more he becomes the controller of his own fate. Passing hastily over the present (for it is a mere nothing by the time-scale we are using), you follow him on into the future. See him in the last Act, though not the last scene, of this great mystery.[31]

The result was: "A race of demigods now rule the planet—and perhaps more than the planet—for eugenics have made certain that only demigods will be born, and psycho-analysis that none of them shall lose or smirch his divinity, and communism that all which divinity requires shall be ready to their hands."[32]

30. Lewis, *They Asked for a Paper*, 155.

31. West, *Magician's Twin*, 155.

32. Lewis, *They Asked for a Paper*, 155.

West indicated that Lewis believed modern science did not require the "kind of blind cosmic evolutionism promoted by H. G. Wells and company."[33] Lewis was very concerned about the evil of applying Darwinism to society. He wrote in 1943 that eugenics was part of the false hope that humans can turn this earth into heaven: "So inveterate is their appetite for Heaven that our best method, at this stage, of attaching them to earth is to make them believe that the earth can be turned into Heaven at some future date by politics or eugenics or 'science.'"[34]

Lewis ends the story with the depressing note regarding where the evolution myth eventually leads, namely to orthodox atheism and the end of all life and the universe:

> If the myth stopped at that point, it might be a little bathetic [meaning used so often that the topic has lost interest]. It would lack the highest grandeur of which human imagination is capable. The last scene reverses all. We have the Twilight of the Gods. All this time, silently, unceasingly, out of all reach of human power, Nature, the old enemy, has been steadily gnawing away. The sun will cool—all suns will cool—the whole universe will run down. Life (every form of life) will be banished, without hope of return, from every inch of infinite space. All ends in nothingness, and *universal darkness covers all*.[35]

He summarized the myth, noting that, although the pattern of myth appears to be one of the noblest that can be conceived, in fact it follows "the pattern of many Elizabethan tragedies, where the protagonist's career can be represented by a slowly ascending and then rapidly falling curve. . . . You see him [mankind] climbing up and up, then blazing in his bright meridian, then finally overwhelmed in ruin."[36] He concluded that this

> world-drama appeals to every part of us. The early struggles of the hero (a theme delightfully doubled, played first

33. West, *Magician's Twin*, 21.

34. Lewis, *Screwtape Letters*, 144.

35. Lewis, *They Asked for a Paper*, 153–56.

36. Ibid., 155–56.

> by [animal] life, and then by man) appeals to our generosity. His future exaltation gives scope to a reasonable optimism; for the tragic close is so very distant that you need not often think of it—we work with millions of years. And the tragic close itself just gives that irony, that grandeur, which calls forth our defiance, and without which all the rest might cloy. There is a beauty in this myth . . . some great genius will yet crystallize it before the incessant stream of philosophic change carries it all.[37]

Lewis feels this modern attitude stems mainly from human's attempt to study our own reason for belief, but this attempt is like taking

> out our eyes to look at them. Thus studied, his own reason appears to him as the epiphenomenon which accompanies chemical or electrical events in a cortex which is itself the by-product of a blind evolutionary process. His own logic . . . becomes merely subjective.[38]

Lewis adds that he believes "less than half of what" the evolution myth "tells me about the past, and . . . nothing of what it tells me about the future."[39] Aside from the evolution myth, the only other story of our origins is Christianity. This is the story he spent much of his career writing about and extolling with great success. He also recognized the fact that entropy is lethal to evolution theory:

> Evolution—even if it were what the mass of the people suppose it to be—is only (by astronomical and physical standards) an inconspicuous foreground detail in the picture. The huge background is filled by quite different principles: entropy, degradation, [and] disorganization.[40]

Furthermore, on the subject of evolution versus entropy, Lewis wrote that the "march of all things is from higher to lower," not lower to

37. Ibid., 153–56.
38. Lewis, *Christian Reflections*, 73.
39. Lewis, *They Asked for a Paper*, 156.
40. Lewis, *Christian Reflections*, 58.

higher as both atheistic and theistic evolution teaches.[41] Intelligent design comes up often in Lewis's writing, touching "on the subject of the spreading of man's corruption, wonders if 'the vast astronomical distances may not be God's quarantine precautions.'"[42]

41. Lewis, *God in the Dock*, 209.

42. Lewis, *World's Last Night*. "Religion and Rocketry" essay, 91.

18

Lewis's Concern Fulfilled in the Movement Against Antievolutionists

THE EVIL FORCES OF one novel are centered in a supposedly scientific organization—the National Institute for Coordinated Experiments (NICE)—with a biologist and a psychologist as important, but evil, characters. Some readers have regarded the book as an attack on science. In his reply to Professor J. B. S. Haldane's highly critical article of Lewis,[1] Lewis answered this criticism by explaining just what he was attacking: "Firstly, a certain view about values"[2] "not scientific planning, as Professor Haldane had thought, but the kind of planned society which first Hitler and then European communists had instituted: 'the disciplined cruelty of some ideological oligarchy.'"[3] The article, titled "Auld Hornie, F.R.S.," a name the Scots have given the devil, which was published in a radical leftist magazine titled *Modern Quarterly*, critiques Lewis's *Space Trilogy*. Haldane claims Lewis has many of the facts of science wrong, suggesting that Lewis should have first brushed up on his science before he wrote the trilogy.

Haldane ignores the important fact that the three-part story is freewheeling science fiction based on the Genesis creation story, not science fact. Haldane especially takes umbrage over the fact that there is only one decent scientist in the three books, all the rest are

1. Haldane, "Auld Hornie, F.R.S.," 32–40.

2. Lewis, *On Stories*. "A Reply to Professor Haldane," was published after C. S. Lewis's death and can be found, most recently, in the collection *On Stories: And Other Essays on Literature*, 78; also in Hooper, *C. S. Lewis*.

3. Lewis, *On Stories*, 80.

intolerant or at least science Fascists, a point that will be covered in much more detail in the next chapter. From these novels Haldane concluded that Lewis has contempt for science, a claim to which Lewis has responded in detail, as was covered above, especially as it related to Darwinism. Haldane does admit that "the tale is told with very great skill, and the descriptions of celestial landscapes and of human and nonhuman behavior are often brilliant."[4]

Lewis correctly observed that every "tyrant must begin by claiming to have what his victims respect and to give what they want. The majority in most modern countries respect science and want to be planned; . . . therefore, . . . if any man or group wishes to enslave us it will of course describe itself as "scientific planned democracy."[5] Six years later, Lewis explained in a letter, "Where benevolent planning, armed with political or economic power, becomes wicked is when it tramples on people's rights for the sake of their good."[6] In his *That Hideous Strength* Lewis covers the problem of the control of a few men over all of the rest of men, noting it now appears that

> we now had the power to dig ourselves in as a species for a pretty staggering period, to take control of our destiny. If Science is really given a free hand it can now take over the human race and re-condition it: make man a really efficient animal. . . . Man has got to take charge of Man. That means, remember that some men have got to take charge of the rest.[7]

This attitude reveals "a lack of concern for individuals and their freedom, another concept that Lewis fought for in his writings."[8] He added that naturalism and empiricism by controlling men's views of the universe and each other produced a union of applied science and social planning with the power of government that would result

4. Haldane, "Auld Hornie, F.R.S.," 33.

5. Lewis, *On Stories*, 80.

6. Crowell, "Theme of the Harmful Effects of Science," 49–50.

7. Quoted in Dickerson and O'Hara, *Narnia and the Fields of Arbol*, 223; original in Lewis, *That Hideous Strength*.

8. Crowell, "Theme of the Harmful Effects of Science," 60.

in the loss of freedom and individuality. Consequently, he felt that democracy was necessary to protect men from each other. To help Professor Haldane understand why he was wrong in saying that Lewis thought that "the application of science to human affairs can lead to Hell,"[9] Lewis explained that it was not the application of science which he feared, but application of science with the force of government, no matter what a man's choice might be.[10]

Lewis further added to make this idea clear to Haldane, who was then an active communist, that

> I am a democrat because I believe that no man or group of men is good enough to be trusted with uncontrolled power over others. And the higher the pretensions of such power, the more dangerous I think it both to the rulers and to the subjects. . . . A metaphysic, held by the rulers with the force of a religion, is a bad sign. It forbids them, like the inquisitor [and later Nazis and Communists] to admit any grain of truth in their opponents, it abrogates the rules of ordinary morality, and it gives a seemingly high, super-personal sanction to all the very human passions by which, like other men, the rulers will frequently be educated.[11]

This review of Lewis's position on Darwinism shows how wrong, actually irresponsible, a 1949 statement by Professor Walsh about the creation-evolution controversy was:

> One possible misconception can be quickly brushed aside. Lewis is not anti-scientific in a Fundamentalist sense. He is not troubled by the "conflict between science and religion" for the reason that his theology does not conflict with anything that science has so far discovered or is ever likely to discover. One cannot imagine him voting to prohibit the teaching of evolution in the schools of Britain.[12]

9. Lewis, *On Stories*, 80.
10. Crowell, "Theme of the Harmful Effects of Science," 60.
11. Lewis, *On Stories*, 81.
12. Walsh, *C. S. Lewis*, 129.

19

Some Conclusions

As he read and thought on the matter, Lewis first left atheism and increasingly became opposed to what is today called the theory of evolutionism or Darwinism. In his earliest correspondence with Acworth

> Lewis stated his willingness to accept any theory that does not contradict the fact that "Man has fallen from the state of innocence in which he was created." By 1951, however, he had begun to believe that Acworth might be right, that evolution was "the central and radical lie in the whole web of falsehood that now governs our lives."[1]

In brief, Lewis's conclusion

> about Darwinism as a biological theory changed over time. In the 1940s and 1950s, a friend tried to get him to join a protest movement against it. However, he refused, fearing that association with anti-Darwinists would damage his reputation as a Christian apologist. "When a man has become a popular Apologist," he explained, "he must watch his step. Everyone is on the look out for things that might discredit him." However, privately, by 1959 he had become increasingly skeptical of Darwinism and concerned about its social effects, especially on account of "the fanatical and twisted attitudes of its defenders."[2]

1. Schultz et al., *Encyclopedia of Religion*, 69.
2. O'Leary, *By Design or by Chance?*, 63–64.

When he was active as an apologist, at the very least Lewis was ambivalent about macroevolution, but he always had problems with Darwinism even before he rejected atheism. As Ferngren and Numbers note, "Lewis especially objected to the idea that human reason and an ordered universe could have arisen from the inorganic and irrational."[3] An example of his early ambivalence is, on December 9, 1944, he wrote, "I am not either attacking or defending Evolution. I believe that Christianity can still be believed, even if evolution is true."[4] Lewis was cautious about openly attacking evolution in his early years because:

> Evolution was a creed so pervasive and so deeply held that even to appear to question it was to invite attack. For example, in a vitriolic article the Marxist geneticist J. B. S. Haldane accused Lewis of getting his science wrong and of traducing scientists in his works of science fiction.[5]

He later came to realize that Darwinism was a critical issue "because evolution formed the basis of theories of philosophical naturalism like Haldane's, which had become the dominant secular worldview. Lewis agreed with Acworth regarding evolution 'as *the* central and radical lie in the whole web of falsehood that now governs our lives.'"[6]

This is one reason why, later in his life, "Lewis became increasingly critical of evolutionism and what he called 'the fanatical and twisted attitudes of its defenders.'"[7] Indeed, his works are among the most effective condemnation of both scientism and Darwinism and, at the same time, the most effective philosophical defenses of intelligent design and creationism published in the last century. As Lewis explains, the popular thought

> that improvement is, somehow, a cosmic law: a conception to which the sciences give no support at all. There

3. Ferngren and Numbers, "C. S. Lewis on Creation," 31.
4. Quoted in Ferngren and Numbers, "C. S. Lewis on Creation," 30.
5. Ferngren and Numbers, "C. S. Lewis on Creation," 30.
6. Ibid., 32.
7. Ibid., 30.

> is no general tendency even for organisms to improve. There is no evidence that the mental and moral capacities of the human race have been increased since man became man. And there is certainly no tendency for the universe as a whole to move in any direction which we should call "good" [or more fit as evolution teaches].[8]

Furthermore, from his experience Lewis found that those Christians who accepted evolution, whom he called the "liberals," were often very intolerant:

> In our days it is the "undogmatic" and "liberal" people who call themselves Christians that are most arrogant & intolerant. I expect justice & even courtesy from many Atheists and, much more, from . . . Modernists [but] I have come to take bitterness and rancour as a matter of course [from Liberals].[9]

He made it clear by the terms "evolution" and "liberals" what he was referring to:

> To a layman, it seems obvious that what unites the Evangelical and the Anglo-Catholic against the "Liberal" or "Modernist" is something very clear and momentous, namely, the fact that both [Evangelicals and Anglo-Catholics] are thorough going supernaturalists, who believe in the Creation, the Fall, the Incarnation, the Resurrection, the Second Coming, and the Four Last Things. This unites them not only with one another, but with the Christian religion as understood *ubique et ab omnibus* [everywhere and by all].[10]

This is exactly what creationists and intelligent design supporters stress today. In his later life Lewis was one of the most effective anti-Darwinists of the last century.

Kuehn, in a review of Reppert, concluded that

8. Lewis, *Christian Reflections*, 58.
9. Lewis, *Letters of C. S. Lewis*, rev. ed., 409.
10. Lewis, *God in the Dock*, 336.

> Reppert's work provides cogent support for the validity of Lewis's argument from reason, along with strong refutations of the many critiques leveled against it throughout recent decades. He shows that several of Lewis's critics do not take his evidences seriously on their own terms, instead preferring to dismiss them in favor of historical or biographical ("He wasn't even a professional philosopher!") considerations. He shows that such *ad hominem* Fallacies are particularly egregious in the analyses of Lewis's interactions with Elizabeth Anscombe.[11]

Lewis also feared Government operating in the name of science, opining that this is how tyrannies are produced, explaining that in "every age the men who want us under their thumb . . . will put forward the particular pretension which the hopes and fears of that age render most potent. . . . It has been magic, it has been Christianity. Now it will certainly be science."[12] In support of this conclusion, Dickerson and O'Hara gave several examples of abuses by science, such as Francis Crick, one of the leading scientists today, who wrote in support of eugenics, that some people, presumably the scientists, "should decide some people should have more children and some should have fewer; . . . you have to decide who is to be born."[13]

Lewis also wrote that, although he firmly believed in God, he detests theocracy for the reason that "every Government consists of mere men and is, strictly viewed, a makeshift; if it adds to its commands 'Thus saith the Lord,' it lies, and lies dangerously. On just the same ground I dread government in the name of science. That is how tyrannies come in."[14] The problem is:

> In every age the men who want us under their thumb, if they have any sense, will put forward the particular pretension which the hopes and fears of that age render

11. Kuehn, *Brains, Minds, and Unicorns*, 10.

12. Lewis, *God in the Dock*, 315.

13. Dickerson and O'Hara, *Narnia and the Fields of Arbol*, 226.

14. Lewis, "Willing Slaves of the Welfare State," first published in the *Observer*, July 20.

> most potent. They "cash in." . . . Perhaps the real scientists may not think much of the tyrants' "science"—they didn't think much of Hitler's racial theories or Stalin's biology. But they can be muzzled.[15]

This conclusion has been supported today by science's use of the courts and governments to suppress all criticism of Darwinism. Larson concluded that "Lewis perceived science as the ultimate threat to freedom in modern society."[16] In this Lewis proved correct, at least in reference to the hold that Darwinism, and science, have on society, our government, and, especially, our courts.[17]

As noted in chapter 1, another writer that had a profound influence on Lewis was Sir Arthur Balfour, who summarized his anti-Darwin conclusions into coherent arguments in his two books *The Foundations of Belief* (1895) and *Theism and Humanism* (1915).

Balfour argued that using Darwinism to support the idea that the human mind is a product of blind material causes was self-refuting: "All creeds which refuse to see an intelligent purpose behind the unthinking powers of material nature are intrinsically incoherent. In the order of causation they base reason upon unreason. In the order of logic they involve conclusions which discredit their own premises."[18]

In his *Theism and Humanism* he argued that, to maintain "our highest beliefs and emotions, we must find for them a congruous origin. Beauty must be more than accident. The source of morality must be moral. The source of knowledge must be rational."[19] West concluded that Balfour produced an effective critique of Darwinian and other materialistic accounts of human morality which "he thought destroyed morality by depicting it as the product of processes that are essentially non-moral."[20] No wonder Balfour had such a major influence on Lewis.

15. Ibid.
16. Larson, "C. S. Lewis on Science," 57.
17. Dickerson and O'Hara, *Narnia and the Fields of Arbol.*
18. Balfour, *Theism and Humanism*, 147.
19. Ibid.
20. West, *Magician's Twin*, 129.

We know that Lewis was both very impressed and influenced by Balfour's argument because Lewis "named *Theism and Humanism* as one of the books that influenced his philosophy of life the most."[21] Lewis's debt to Balfour is most obvious in Lewis's book *Miracles: A Preliminary Study*, where he noted that modern materialists argue that the "mental behavior we now call rational thinking or inference must . . . have been 'evolved' by natural selection, by the gradual weeding out of types less fitted to survive."[22] Lewis then argued against this conclusion by materialists and "flatly denied that such a Darwinian process could have produced human rationality."[23] In support of this view, Lewis wrote that natural

> selection could operate only by eliminating responses that were biologically hurtful and multiplying those which tended to survival. But it is not conceivable that any improvement of responses could ever turn them into acts of insight, or even remotely tend to do so. Why not? Because "[t]he relation between response and stimulus is utterly different from that between knowledge and the truth known."[24]

Following Balfour, "Lewis held that attributing the development of human reason to a non-rational process like natural selection ends up undermining our confidence in reason itself."[25] This same logic was used by Notre Dame Professor Alvin Plantinga to defend theism. West adds that Lewis, in his book

> *Miracles* rejected a Darwinian explanation for the human mind because it undermined the validity of reason, he rejected a Darwinian account of morality because it would undermine the authority of morality by attributing it to an essentially amoral process of survival of the fittest.[26]

21. Ibid.
22. Lewis, *Miracles*, 27–28.
23. West, *Magician's Twin*, 25.
24. Ibid.; Lewis, *Miracles*, 28.
25. West, *Magician's Twin*, 25.
26. Ibid.

Lewis would hardly be called a Darwinist, or even an evolutionist, today. That which Orthodox Darwinism explained as due purely to the natural selection of mutations, including mind, body and morality, Lewis explained is due to divine creation by God.

The Anti-Darwinian Argument during His Lifetime

Some naïve readers might get the impression that Lewis knew as much about the origins debate as we know now. The scientific argument against evolution in Lewis's lifetime was very thin. It is remarkable that Lewis managed to take his argument as far as he did. Morris and Whitcomb's *Genesis Flood* (1961) was published before Lewis died, but we have no reason to believe that Lewis even heard of it. One must wonder what he would have made of it if he did. It's hard to tell how he would have reacted. It would seem likely he had only mostly Acworth's writings and correspondence to work with, plus Balfour's criticisms as well as his own (philosophical) skepticism. An organization formally titled *The Evolution Protest Movement* existed in his day, but was very small and its influence was very limited. Furthermore, the creation movement in America was also then very small and limited to certain churches.

Bibliography

Aeschliman, Michael D. *The Restitution of Man: C. S. Lewis and the Case against Scientism*. Grand Rapids: Eerdmans, 1998.

Ayala, Francisco J. "Darwin's Greatest Discovery: Design without Designer." *Proceedings of the National Academy of Science* 104 (2007) 8567–73.

Balfour, Arthur J. *Theism and Humanism: The Book That Influenced C. S. Lewis*. Edited by Michael Perry. Seattle: Inkling, 2000.

Beavan, Colin. *Fingerprints: The Origins of Crime Detection and the Murder Case That Launched Forensic Science*. New York: Hyperion, 2001.

Bergman, Jerry. "Creative Evolution: An Anti-Darwin Theory Won a Nobel." *Impact* 409 (2007) 1–4. Also as: *Acts & Facts* 36 (2007). http://www.icr.org/article/creative-evolution-anti-darwin-theory-won-nobel.

———. *Slaughter of the Dissidents: The Shocking Truth about Killing the Careers of Darwin Doubters*. Rev. ed. Southworth, WA: Leafcutter, 2012.

Bergman, Jerry, and Joseph Calkins. "Why the Inverted Human Retina Is a Superior Design." *CRSQ* 45(3) (2009) 213–24.

Bergson, Henri. *Creative Evolution*. New York: Random House, 1944.

Beversluis, John. "Beyond the Double Bolted Door." *Christian History* 4 (1985) 28–31. https://www.christianhistoryinstitute.org/magazine/article/beyond-the-double-bolted-door.

Bredvold, Louis I. "The Achievement of C. S. Lewis." *Intercollegiate Review* 4 (1968) 116–22.

Bloom, Herald. *C. S. Lewis*. Bloom's Modern Critical Views. New York: Chelsea House, 2006.

Chesterton, G. K. *The Everlasting Man*. London: Hodder & Stoughton, 1925.

Collins, C. John. *Did Adam and Eve Really Exist? Who They Were and Why You Should Care*. Wheaton, IL: Crossway, 2011.

Como, James T., ed. *C. S. Lewis at the Breakfast Table and Other Reminiscences*. New ed. San Diego: Harcourt, Brace, 1992.

Crowell, Faye Ann. "The Theme of the Harmful Effects of Science in the Works of C. S. Lewis." MA thesis, Texas A & M University, 1971.

Cunningham, Richard. *Defender of the Faith*. Eugene, OR: Wipf & Stock, 2008.

Darwin, Charles. *The Correspondence of Charles Darwin.* Vol. 7, *1858–1859.* Cambridge: Cambridge University Press, 1991.

———. *The Correspondence of Charles Darwin.* Vol. 9, *1861.* Cambridge: Cambridge University Press, 1994.

———. *The Descent of Man and Selection in Relation to Sex.* London, 1871.

———. *The Origin of Species.* Vol. 1. 6th ed. New York, 1897.

Dawkins, Richard. *The Blind Watchmaker.* New York: Norton, 1986.

———. *The God Delusion.* Boston: Houghton Mifflin, 2006.

Deasy, Philip. "God, Space, and C. S. Lewis." *Commonweal* 68 (1958) 421–23.

Dickerson, Matthew, and David O'Hara. *Narnia and the Fields of Arbol: The Environmental Vision of C. S. Lewis.* Lexington: University Press of Kentucky, 2009.

Dobzhansky, Theodosius. "Changing Man." *Science,* 155(3761) (1967) 409–15.

Dorsett, Lyle. "C. S. Lewis: A Profile of His Life." *Christian History* 4 (1985) 6–11. https://www.christianhistoryinstitute.org/magazine/article/c-s-lewis-a-profile.

Duriez, Colin. *The A–Z of C. S. Lewis: A Complete Guide to His Life, Thoughts and Writings.* Oxford: Lion Hudson, 2013.

Evans, C. Stephen. "A Body Blow to Darwinist Materialism Courtesy of the Great C. S. Lewis." Review of *C. S. Lewis's Dangerous Idea,* by Victor Reppert. *Book Service* (one-page flyer), 2004. A copy is in the author's files.

Ferngren, G. B, and Ronald L. Numbers. "C. S. Lewis on Creation and Evolution: The Acworth Letters, 1944–1960." *American Scientific Affiliation* 49 (1996) 28–34.

Frankl, Victor. "'Nothing But—' On Reductionism and Nihilism." *Encounter* 33 (1969) 51–61.

Fuller, Edmond. *Books with Men behind Them.* New York: Random House, 1962.

Gardner, Martin. *Fads & Fallacies in the Name of Science.* New York: Dover, 1957.

Gibb, Jocelyn. *Light on C. S. Lewis.* London: Bles, 1965.

Glyer, Diana Pavlac. *The Company They Keep: C. S. Lewis and J. R. R. Tolkien as Writers in Community.* Kent, OH: Kent State University Press, 2007.

Green, Roger Lancelyn. *C. S. Lewis.* London: Bodley Head, 1963.

Green, Roger Lancelyn, and Roger Hooper. *C. S. Lewis: A Biography.* New York: Harcourt, Brace, 1974.

Gruber, Howard E. *Darwin on Man: A Psychological Study of Scientific Creativity.* 2nd ed. Chicago: University of Chicago Press, 1974.

Haldane, J. B. S. "Auld Hornie, F.R.S." *Modern Quarterly* (1946) 32–40.

Hart, Dabney. "Teacher, Historian, Critic, Apologist." *Christian History* 4 (1985) 21–24. https://www.christianhistoryinstitute.org/magazine/article/lewis-teacher-historian-critic-apologist.

Hooper, Walter, ed. *C. S. Lewis: A Companion & Guide.* London: HarperCollins, 1996.

Huxley, Julian. "Evolution and Genetics." In *What Is Science?*, edited by James R. Newman, 256–89. New York: Simon and Schuster, 1955.

Irvine, William. "The Influence of Darwin on Literature." *Proceedings of the American Philosophical Society* 103 (1959) 616–28.

Kilby, Clyde S. *The Christian World of C. S. Lewis*. Grand Rapids: Eerdmans, 1964.

———. "Into the Land of Imagination." *Christian History* 4 (1985) 16–18. http://www.christianitytoday.com/history/issues/issue-7/into-land-of-imagination.html.

Kreeft, Peter. "Western Civilizations at the Crossroads." *Christian History* 4 (1985) 25–26. https://www.christianhistoryinstitute.org/magazine/article/at-the-crossroads.

Kuehn, K. "Brains, Minds, and Unicorns: A Critical Review of Victor Reppert's *C. S. Lewis's Dangerous Idea*." Paper originally located at the University of California, Irvine, Department of Physical Sciences website, 2004. No longer available. A copy is in the author's files.

Larson, Edward S. "C. S. Lewis on Science as a Threat to Freedom." In *The Magician's Twin: C. S. Lewis on Science, Scientism, and Society*, edited by John G. West, 53–58. Seattle: Discovery Institute, 2012.

Larson, Edward J., and Larry Witham. "Leading Scientists Still Reject God." *Nature* 394 (1998) 313.

Lazo, Andrew, and Mary Anne Phemister, eds. *Mere Christians: Inspiring Stories of Encounters with C. S. Lewis*. Grand Rapids: Baker, 2009.

Levine, Joseph S., and Kenneth R. Miller. *Biology: Discovering Life*. 2nd ed. Lexington, MA: Heath, 1994.

Lewis, C. S. *The Abolition of Man: Or, Reflections on Education with Special Reference to the Teaching of English in the Upper Forms of Schools*. New York: Macmillan, 1965.

———. *The Business of Heaven*. London: Fount Paperbacks, 1984.

———. *Christian Reflections*. Grand Rapids: Eerdmans, 1967.

———. *The Collected Letters of C. S. Lewis*. Vol. 1, *Family Letters, 1905–1931*. New York: HarperSanFrancisco, 2004.

———. *The Collected Letters of C. S. Lewis*. Vol., 2, *Books, Broadcasts, and the War 1931–1949*. New York: HarperSanFrancisco, 2004.

———. *The Collected Letters of C. S. Lewis*. Vol., 3, *Narnia, Cambridge, and Joy 1950–1963*. New York: HarperSanFrancisco, 2007.

———. *The Collected Works of C. S. Lewis: The Pilgrim's Regress, Christian Reflections, God in the Dock*. New York: Inspirational, 1996.

———. "De Descriptione Temporum." In *C. S. Lewis: Selected Literary Essays*, edited by Walter Hooper, 1–14. Cambridge: Cambridge University Press, 1969.

———. *The Discarded Image*. Cambridge: Cambridge University Press, 1964.

———. *English Literature in the Sixteenth Century*. New York: Clarendon, 1954.

———. [Nat Whilk, pseud.]. "Evolution Hymn." *Cambridge Review* 78 (1957) 227.

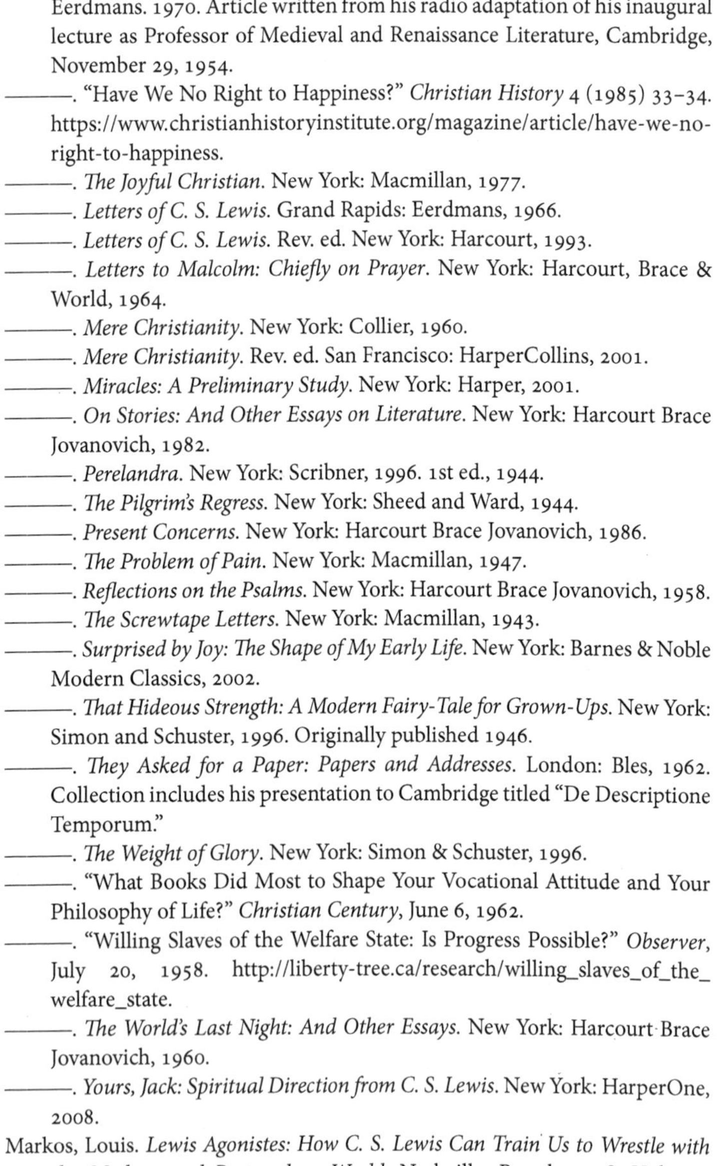

———. *God in the Dock: Essays on Theology and Ethics*. Grand Rapids: Eerdmans. 1970. Article written from his radio adaptation of his inaugural lecture as Professor of Medieval and Renaissance Literature, Cambridge, November 29, 1954.

———. "Have We No Right to Happiness?" *Christian History* 4 (1985) 33–34. https://www.christianhistoryinstitute.org/magazine/article/have-we-no-right-to-happiness.

———. *The Joyful Christian*. New York: Macmillan, 1977.

———. *Letters of C. S. Lewis*. Grand Rapids: Eerdmans, 1966.

———. *Letters of C. S. Lewis*. Rev. ed. New York: Harcourt, 1993.

———. *Letters to Malcolm: Chiefly on Prayer*. New York: Harcourt, Brace & World, 1964.

———. *Mere Christianity*. New York: Collier, 1960.

———. *Mere Christianity*. Rev. ed. San Francisco: HarperCollins, 2001.

———. *Miracles: A Preliminary Study*. New York: Harper, 2001.

———. *On Stories: And Other Essays on Literature*. New York: Harcourt Brace Jovanovich, 1982.

———. *Perelandra*. New York: Scribner, 1996. 1st ed., 1944.

———. *The Pilgrim's Regress*. New York: Sheed and Ward, 1944.

———. *Present Concerns*. New York: Harcourt Brace Jovanovich, 1986.

———. *The Problem of Pain*. New York: Macmillan, 1947.

———. *Reflections on the Psalms*. New York: Harcourt Brace Jovanovich, 1958.

———. *The Screwtape Letters*. New York: Macmillan, 1943.

———. *Surprised by Joy: The Shape of My Early Life*. New York: Barnes & Noble Modern Classics, 2002.

———. *That Hideous Strength: A Modern Fairy-Tale for Grown-Ups*. New York: Simon and Schuster, 1996. Originally published 1946.

———. *They Asked for a Paper: Papers and Addresses*. London: Bles, 1962. Collection includes his presentation to Cambridge titled "De Descriptione Temporum."

———. *The Weight of Glory*. New York: Simon & Schuster, 1996.

———. "What Books Did Most to Shape Your Vocational Attitude and Your Philosophy of Life?" *Christian Century*, June 6, 1962.

———. "Willing Slaves of the Welfare State: Is Progress Possible?" *Observer*, July 20, 1958. http://liberty-tree.ca/research/willing_slaves_of_the_welfare_state.

———. *The World's Last Night: And Other Essays*. New York: Harcourt Brace Jovanovich, 1960.

———. *Yours, Jack: Spiritual Direction from C. S. Lewis*. New York: HarperOne, 2008.

Markos, Louis. *Lewis Agonistes: How C. S. Lewis Can Train Us to Wrestle with the Modern and Postmodern World*. Nashville: Broadman & Holman, 2003.

———. *On the Shoulders of Hobbits: The Road to Virtue with Tolkien and Lewis*. Chicago: Moody, 2012.

———. *Restoring Beauty: The Good, the True, and the Beautiful in the Writings of C. S. Lewis*. Downers Grove: InterVarsity, 2010.

Markos, Louis, and David Diener. *C. S. Lewis: An Apologist for Education*. Camp Hill, PA: Classical Academic, 2015.

Martindale, W., and J. Root. ed. *The Quotable Lewis*. Wheaton, IL: Tyndale, 1990.

McGrath, Alister. *C. S. Lewis: A Life*. Carol Stream, IL: Tyndale, 2013.

Moore, James. *The Post-Darwinian Controversies*. New York: Cambridge University Press, 1979.

Murphy, Brian. *C. S. Lewis*. Starmont Reader's Guide 14. Mercer Island, WA: Starmont, 1983.

Nicholi, Armand M. *The Question of God: C. S. Lewis and Sigmund Freud Debate God, Love, Sex, and the Meaning of Life*. New York: Free Press, 2002.

Numbers, Ronald L. *The Creationists: From Scientific Creationism to Intelligent Design*. Cambridge: Harvard University Press, 2006.

O'Leary, Denyse. *By Design or By Chance?* Kitchener, ON: Castle Quay, 2004.

Peterson, Michael L. "C. S. Lewis on Evolution and Intelligent Design." *Perspectives on Science and Christian Faith* 62 (2010) 253–66.

Poe, Harry Lee, and Rebecca Whitten Poe, eds. *C. S. Lewis Remembered: Collected Reflections of Students, Friends & Colleagues*. Grand Rapids: Zondervan, 2006.

Rainer, Tom S. *Surprising Insights from the Unchurched and Proven Ways to Reach Them*. Grand Rapids: Zondervan, 2001.

Raymond, E. T. *A Life of Arthur James Belford*. Boston: Little, Brown, 1920.

Reid, Daniel G. *Dictionary of Christianity in America*. Downers Grove: InterVarsity, 1990.

Reppert, Victor. *C. S. Lewis's Dangerous Idea*. Downers Grove: InterVarsity, 2003.

Roberts, Adam. *Silk and Potatoes: Contemporary Arthurian Fantasy*. Atlanta: Rodopi, 1998.

Sagan, Carl. *Cosmos*. New York: Random House, 1980.

Santamaria, Abigail. *Joy: Poet, Seeker, and the Women Who Captivated C. S. Lewis*. Boston: Houghton Mifflin Harcourt, 2015.

Schaefer, Henry F. *Science and Christianity: Conflict or Coherence?* Athens, GA: University of Georgia, 2003.

Schmerl, Rudolf. "Reason's Dream: Anti-Totalitarian Themes and Techniques of Fantasy." PhD diss., University of Michigan, 1960.

Schultz, Jeffery, et al., eds. *Encyclopedia of Religion in American Politics*. Santa Barbara, CA: Greenwood, 1998.

Shermer, Michael. *How We Believe*. New York: Freeman, 2000.

Tolson, J. "God's Storyteller: The Curious Life and Prodigious Influence of C. S. Lewis, the Man behind *The Chronicles of Narnia*." *U.S. News & World Report* 139 (2005) 46–52.

Tomkins, Jeff, and Jerry Bergman. "Is the Human Genome Nearly Identical to Chimpanzee?—A Reassessment of the Literature." *Journal of Creation* 25 (2012) 54–60.

Turner, J. Scott. *The Tinker's Accomplice: How Design Emerges from Life Itself.* Cambridge: Harvard University Press, 2007.

Walsh, Chad. *C. S. Lewis: Apostle to the Skeptics.* New York: Macmillan, 1949.

Weikart, Richard. "C. S. Lewis and Science." *Credo Magazine*, 2012. http://www.credomag.com/2012/10/24/c-s-lewis-and-science.

West, John G., ed. *The Magician's Twin: C. S. Lewis on Science, Scientism, and Society.* Seattle: Discovery Institute, 2012.

White, William Luther. *The Image of Man in C. S. Lewis.* Nashville: Abingdon, 1969.

Wielenberg, Erick. *God and the Reach of Reason: C. S. Lewis, David Hume, and Bertrand Russell.* New York: Cambridge University Press, 2008.

Wile, Jay L. "Everyone Wants a Piece of C. S. Lewis." July 15, 2011. http://blog.drwile.com/?p=5550.

Williams, C., and C. S. Lewis. *Taliessin through Logres, The Region of the Summer Stars, Arthurian Torso.* Grand Rapids: Eerdmans, 1974.

Williams, Donald. *Mere Humanity: G. K. Chesterton, C. S. Lewis, and J. R. R. Tolkien on the Human Condition.* Nashville: B&H, 2006.

Wilson, A. N. *C. S. Lewis: A Biography.* London: Collins, 1990.

Yancey, Philip. *What Good Is God?* New York: Faith Words, 2010.

Made in the USA
Middletown, DE
16 July 2018